About the Author

Tina Murphy started her Run With Tina courses not as a business idea but from a desire to help other women learn to love running as she does. She is a qualified fitness instructor, a lifelong yoga student and interested in all aspects of fitness, nutrition and well-being. She often draws on her own experiences in overcoming her struggles with food and fitting exercise into a busy lifestyle. Her courses have helped hundreds of women transform their lives.

slim
with tina

The easy way to lose weight and keep it off

Tina Murphy

MERCIER PRESS
IRISH PUBLISHER – IRISH STORY

For more information and 10 per cent off all 'Run with Tina' and 'Slim with Tina' courses go to www.runwithtina.com and use the code BOOK10

MERCIER PRESS
Cork
www.mercierpress.ie

ISBN: 978 1 78117 313 8

10 9 8 7 6 5 4 3 2 1

Printed and bound in the EU.

CONTENTS

LIST OF RECIPES

BREAKFASTS

BRUNCH

SMOOTHIES

SIDES

MAIN MEALS

DESSERTS

INTRODUCTION

Some years ago I found myself unemployed and in need of something to do to fill my time while I looked for a new job. I had always wanted to work in fitness and as I had recently started running again, after years of intensive yoga study, I decided to start teaching a group of women how to run. I felt I had something new to offer people who were desperate to get fit but didn't know where to start. At first it was just a hobby that I did for free because it was fun and exactly the kind of new challenge I needed. However, after a while word got around and more and more women wanted to join my group. As the country was gripped by recession and it seemed unlikely I was going to find a job any time soon, I decided I might as well try to turn this hobby into a business, and so Run with Tina was born. Today, with help from a great team of instructors, I've transformed over 2,000 women from couch potatoes into runners and, more importantly, into people who enjoy exercise.

Listening to the clients in my classes, it soon became obvious that people also wanted to find a better way to lose weight – whatever they had been doing so far wasn't working long term and there was a lot of confusion over what you should and shouldn't do. So I teamed up with nutritionist Elaine O'Gorman and we came up with the Slim with Tina plan, which was very much based on the same principles as Run with Tina – a simple, straightforward plan that's suitable for normal women with busy lifestyles.

A problem I face daily is that people equate healthy eating with weight loss, and anything that doesn't cause you to put on weight is considered healthy. However, this is not true. Some of the worst things you can eat or drink have no calories at all and thus are seen as diet-friendly foods, whereas some of the most nutritious foods are high in fat and calories and often avoided by dieters. Many popular diets are, in fact, extremely unhealthy, requiring you to leave out complete food groups while eating excessive amounts of others, or making you cut calories drastically. Yet they're all sold on the promise of healthy weight loss and very few dieters question these claims.

My aim, therefore, with the Slim with Tina programme is to go back to basics and give you straightforward information on what is healthy and what isn't, why you need to eat all food groups (including the dreaded carbohydrates) and why fat can actually help you to lose weight. This is not new information, but it has been forgotten because of the focus on losing weight and losing it fast.

This book is based on my popular Slim with Tina plan, which has transformed hundreds of women's lives and bodies over the last year. This book will help you bring your focus back to health, not just weight loss, and you'll be surprised to find how easy losing weight is once you have achieved this. It will help you change the way you see food, educate you about what you should be eating, and also show you how simple lifestyle changes can have a huge impact on your well-being. If you stick with it, by this time next year your life will have changed for the better.

Enjoy the process and be good to yourself!

1
GETTING STARTED

In this chapter you'll learn:

- How to use your dieting history to learn from your mistakes.

- Why diets don't work.

- How to take stock of your current lifestyle.

- How to set goals.

- Happy-weight visualisation.

- How to reach your goals.

The Slim with Tina plan is not just about following a food plan for a number of weeks to lose weight and simply doing what the plan says. The aim here is to change the way you see food for good and to teach you why some foods are good for you and others are not, what is in the food you consume and what your body actually needs. This will help you not only to lose weight but also to be healthy and strong. More importantly, you will learn to understand your own relationship with food – why you eat and why it is so hard to get it right.

I am hoping that you, like so many of my clients, will come to see your food, health and weight in a completely different light. After you've finished this book, you won't need to go on another diet, because you will have all the tools and knowledge to decide for yourself what is good for you and what isn't; which foods lead to weight loss and which to weight gain. Your relationship with food will have improved so that it will be easy to maintain a balanced diet where you can have a little treat here and there. You will also start to improve your lifestyle – I say 'start' because these things take time. You need to take it easy in order to make lasting changes, whether that means getting more sleep, being more active, changing your attitude or accepting yourself as you are. So let's get started.

GETTING TO KNOW YOURSELF

At the root of this plan is changing your relationship with food, the way you feel about it and the way you feel about diets. The best way to do this is to look back at what you've tried so far, particularly at what hasn't worked. Your failures and mistakes are the best teachers.

If you're anything like the majority of my clients, you'll have tried a few diets in the past, but since you're reading this book I'm guessing that none of them has worked long term. Recognising what went wrong will help you ensure that you don't make the same mistakes again and that you stop the never-ending cycle of yo-yo dieting, going from one fad diet to the next.

You might be impatient to get to the plan as quickly as possible, but before you do, it is important that you learn to understand your past relationship with food, why you eat what you do and what foods you should and shouldn't be eating. This will make it much easier to follow the plan when you get there.

The first step is to take the time to do the following exercise properly – it will be a real eye-opener and will make changing your habits easier. Make sure you have enough time to write your answers down, and please make sure you are honest with yourself.

Exercise: Previous Diets

Read each of the steps and write down the answers to each question.

Step 1:

List all the diets you've tried and for each one make a note of:

- What was it, e.g. high protein; meal replacement; counting points?

- How long did you stay on the plan?

- Why did you stop?

- Did you lose any weight?

- Did you keep it off?

- Why do you think the diet didn't work?

- Anything else special you remember about the diet.

Step 2:

- Have you ever fallen off the wagon while following a diet plan? More than once? How did you react? How did you feel?

- If you managed to follow the plan long enough to lose weight and then gained the weight back, how did this make you feel?

- If you've tried many diets and never succeeded, how does this make you feel about yourself?

Step 3:

- Why do you think none of the diets above worked?

- Did you get anything positive out of any of them?

Step 4:

- How do you feel about diets now?

- How do you feel about your ability to lose weight? Do you think you can do it? Can you imagine yourself ever being happy with your weight?

When I do this exercise with my clients, the stories are always similar. Everyone has tried one diet after another and yet here they are, back at square one. We often have a bit of a laugh at the silly diets we've tried (cabbage soup diet, anyone?) and the mind games we've played to cheat the system (such as not eating all day on the day of your weigh-in and then heading straight out for a pizza afterwards) without realising that we're only cheating ourselves. And yet many people keep going back to the same programmes or trying new crazy diets, one after another, with the same results – they lose weight but it won't stay off. What's worse is that they can end up feeling guilty for cheating on a diet, feeling like a failure for not being able to stick to the plan and completely losing faith in their ability to ever lose the weight. They think that they just don't have the will-power and will always fail, but they keep trying anyway and each time they fail their belief that they will never be able to lose the weight becomes a little stronger.

If you've had this experience you might have decided that you'll never go on another diet again; what's the point? Then you see an ad for the next miracle diet that promises you'll lose a stone in two weeks and you decide to give it one more try. Advertisers know how desperate women are to lose weight and to look like the (photoshopped) models in the ads. What's more, they know you want immediate results. So even though in the back of your mind you know that fad diets don't work, you sign up because they say it's 'revolutionary', it's been developed by some doctor and it's based on some science that makes it better than the others. You convince yourself that last time you just weren't focused and dedicated enough, but this time you're really going to do it, you're going to be fully committed and work hard. And then, after a week of eating nothing but spinach, celery and poached chicken, you fall off the wagon and order a takeaway … and the cycle begins again. Makes you feel really crap, doesn't it?

Well, I have news for you; it's not you, it's the diets, and you are certainly not alone in this – most women can relate to you. That girl up the road who lost two stone on Atkins or one of its many variations – she'll have put it back on with an extra half stone by this time next year. The good news is that with the right tools you can and WILL lose that weight once and for all, and you're going to love not just the results but also the actual process, so stop being so hard on yourself. Chin up!

WHY DON'T DIETS WORK?

Every few months a new diet comes out, each backed by doctors and science, telling us what the best way to lose weight is. They all claim to be the only effective way to lose weight, and yet their conflicting theories only serve to confuse things further.

Over the years I have spoken to hundreds of women whose stories are all pretty much the same. The main problem that these fad diets have created is that they have left people very confused over what is healthy and what isn't; what you should and shouldn't eat. There is so much conflicting information and so much questionable, and in many cases bad, advice out there that it is hard to know who to trust. In the next few chapters I will remove this confusion, but first let's look at the key points of why diets don't work.

1. Diets are too strict and too negative

Most diets are very strict, making them impossible to follow for normal people with busy lives. When you're on them there are so many things you are not allowed to eat that sticking to them requires a lot of will-power. Furthermore, the mindset tends to be very negative – the whole plan is based on what you *cannot* have, putting you in a negative frame of mind and making all the banned things seem even more tempting.

When the plan gets too much and you give in to temptation and have something from the long list of banned goodies because you *just need something*, then you feel like, 'This is so typical. I can never stick to anything. I always do this.'

After a few weeks of this, is it any wonder most people give up? And after a few experiences like this, you start believing you're just not strong enough to ever lose the weight.

2. Unrealistic expectations

People these days want everything now, with as little effort as possible. This is the world we live in – everything is instant; we are busy, we don't have time to wait. So who has ten weeks to lose 10lbs? You have to drop that dress size in a week. Realistically, this is not going to happen, and if it does, it's not going to last. Most often, when it doesn't happen people get frustrated and lose motivation – 'What's the point of making all this effort when I'm not losing a dress size in a week?'

Marketers know all this, so diets have to offer fast results for them to sell – but what they don't tell you is that in order for you to achieve fast results, you will have to go on a seriously restrictive diet that is not sustainable, and that it is unlikely you'll keep the weight off once you finish the programme.

Recently, I sent copy for an ad to our graphic designer. One line read 'lose up to 16lbs in 8 weeks'. I was a bit nervous about including this line because I do not like to promise people that they will lose x amount of weight – this depends on so many things. Everyone is different. For starters, someone with 200lbs to lose will lose 20lbs fast and relatively easily, but for someone with only 30lbs to lose it will happen much more slowly, so it is difficult to make a generalisation. Also, I like to get people to focus on things other than the scales. However, bookings for our new online weight-loss programme, which we were marketing as a healthy way to lose weight, were very slow (healthy is good but, let's face it, weight/looks are a bigger concern these days), so we had to come up with new material to get people's attention. Very soon our designer emailed back. 'Hey, just wanted to check, is that right, 16lbs in 8 weeks? Is that all?' Yes, it is all and I had thought it was a good result for eight weeks; in fact, I thought I was over-promising a bit, as many people wouldn't lose that amount. It's based on a loss of 2lbs per week, which is the maximum you should lose in a week to be safe and sustainable. Even 1lb per week is great. But very often, this just isn't enough for people and I find this frustrating. I am forever having to reassure clients that just because they lost only 1lb this week, they haven't failed. In fact, they're doing great; they're losing weight at a very healthy rate and they don't even feel like they're on a diet – what could be better than that?

The reason people expect fast results is because that's what most diets promise, but if you want fast results you can't expect these to be sustainable or healthy.

3. Diets are not sustainable long term

When you do manage to get to your target weight following a diet, then what? Most people go back to their old ways, because no one wants to be on a diet forever. And once the dieting stops it is more common for people to put the weight back on than to keep it off. But why is it so hard to keep off? Because, as we have already established, diets are too strict; they are based on limiting what you eat, limiting calories or cutting out whole food groups so that you get fast, drastic results. This is obviously not sustainable, nor is it healthy in the long term; the focus is all on weight loss rather than health. Some diets have maintenance plans, but these are based on the same principle and again are not sustainable in the long term.

When you take a more sensible, though slower, approach and learn about nutrition, learn to understand yourself and why you eat, address emotional eating and your relationship with food, you will create lifelong habits and a completely new lifestyle. Although you might be on this plan forever, it won't feel like a plan (I know right now it might seem difficult to believe that you won't miss all the nice foods, but trust me, the way you see and feel about food will completely change and it's all good). For those of you with children, an additional bonus will be that your whole family will develop healthier eating habits for life.

4. Diets focus on weight (and looks) only

One of the biggest problems with diets, in my opinion, is that they are purely focused on getting you to your target weight. They give you no other incentive to eat certain foods (or to avoid others) and no other way to measure your success. Furthermore, the focus is usually on looks – on how your body will look so much better (implying that it's not good enough now), you'll have this great beach body, everyone will be jealous and so on.

Of course we all want to look great, but weight loss and looks, I've found, are poor motivators. For starters, many people look great carrying a bit of extra weight. In fact, some people look better when they're overweight. Many use this as a reason not to lose weight – 'I think I look better with a bit of extra weight on' (yes, you do) – but let's face it, it's not healthy. The worst reason ever is the excuse that 'men prefer women with some curves'; so you're saying you stay at an unhealthy weight because you want to please men? Your health should be more important than how you look or, indeed, what men think.

It really frustrates me when the focus is all on looks – weight should first and foremost be a health issue; there is a mountain of evidence about the long-term risks of being overweight. To truly stay motivated you need to focus on other things – how you feel, physically and mentally, how your life has improved, how happy you are with yourself, and health indicators such as lowered cholesterol levels or blood pressure. These are the benefits you will be able to achieve almost immediately, and noticing them is very important for motivation – we will talk more about these later.

Being overweight puts you at higher risk of health problems such as:

- Cardiovascular disease (heart disease and stroke)
- Type 2 diabetes
- High blood pressure
- Cancer
- Musculoskeletal disorders such as osteoarthritis

- Kidney disease
- Complications in pregnancy.

5. Diets don't work on your attitude

Most diets do not address your attitude. I find this surprising, because being in the right frame of mind is the key to success in anything – this has been proven over and over. With the right attitude you can achieve anything. As I mentioned earlier, diets focus on what you're not allowed to have. They want you to 'be strong', resist temptation, and the only reward is looking fabulous at the end. Talking about success and failure already implies it's going to be really hard – and since no one wants to fail, the pressure is on. I am a huge believer in the power of your mind – if you tell yourself something is going to be hard, of course it's going to be hard. In fact it will quite likely be impossible – only the strongest will reach their goal.

It's really important to work on your attitude. Do not start this plan thinking it's going to be hard, because it's not; it's going to require some work and some commitment, but it's not going to be impossible. You will enjoy it and when it does feel a bit tough you just need to remember how great you'll feel tomorrow for making the effort to cook this healthy dinner tonight. It's all in your head; you need to start thinking positive and turning negatives into positives; see the silver lining, the glass half full. You are taking control of your health and looking after yourself, treating yourself with the respect you deserve. Plus you're going to discover lots of new exciting foods and tastes and you will notice many health benefits and improvements in your life – you should feel excited about this!

6. Diets don't address emotional eating

From speaking to hundreds of women, it is obvious to me that the biggest obstacle to weight loss is the reason we eat. Overcoming emotional eating and consequently changing your relationship with food is the key to losing weight relatively easily and keeping it off. This is such an important topic, but it is often overlooked by weight-loss plans and experts. I believe that if you address emotional eating, along with your attitude, you will be able to eat what you want and keep the weight off without having to use an awful lot of will-power. We will talk more about emotions and attitude in the next chapter.

I hope by this point you are able to see why all those diets you've tried in the past haven't worked, and if going from one diet to another made you lose confidence in your ability to stick to a plan and lose the weight, I hope you are starting to get back some of that confidence and the belief that you *can* do it.

SELF-ASSESSMENT

Now we've established why what you've done so far didn't work, let's look at where you are right now.

Overleaf is a Slim with Tina self-check exercise that I get my clients to do regularly. However, the most important time to do this is before you start.

Look at the statements and rate each one on a scale of 1 to 10, with 10 being strongly agree and 1 being strongly disagree. In other words, the higher your score is the better. As the weeks go on and you improve you diet and lifestyle, your scores should naturally start going up.

LIFESTYLE	W1	W2	W4	W6	W8	W10
I get enough sleep						
The quality of my sleep is great						
My life is stress free						
I enjoy my life						
I have enough me-time						
I feel fit						
I don't get out of breath easily						
I am active						
I'm at a healthy weight						
My immune system is great (I am rarely sick)						

INSIDE YOUR HEAD	W1	W2	W4	W6	W8	W10
I feel self-confident						
I'm always happy (never feel down)						
I don't let things get to me						
My concentration is great						
I am motivated						
My thoughts are mostly positive						
I always think positively of myself						
I love and respect myself						

YOUR BODY	W1	W2	W4	W6	W8	W10
I am happy with my weight						
I am happy with my size and shape						

My skin is clear and healthy						
My body is free of aches and pains						
I don't suffer from heartburn						
I don't suffer from IBS						
I never feel bloated						
I don't suffer from any other digestive problems						
I don't suffer from food cravings (sugar, junk, etc.)						

YOUR DIET	W1	W2	W4	W6	W8	W10
I eat 2 portions of fruit daily						
I eat at least 3 portions of vegetables daily						
I eat carbohydrates at every meal						
I eat protein at every meal						
I eat healthy fats daily						
I drink 2–3 litres of water daily						
I never eat takeaways						
I never eat ready meals						
I never eat sugar (excluding fresh fruit)						
I never eat pastries, cakes or biscuits						
I never eat wheat						
I never drink fizzy drinks						
I never drink alcohol						
I never consume caffeine						

YOUR EATING HABITS	W1	W2	W4	W6	W8	W10
I have breakfast every day						
I eat regularly (3 meals and 2 snacks per day)						
I always have time to plan my meals						
I never overeat						
I never binge eat						
I cook most of my meals myself						

How did you score? Highlight any statements where you scored below 5; these are the areas you want to work to improve. If you see a lot of areas that need work, it's best to prioritise. What would you like to fix first? You will also find that once you start working on one area, others improve too, and when you start eating healthier, a lot of these things will fix themselves, so don't feel overwhelmed if there's a lot of work to be done.

Filling in this table every couple of weeks will really help you stay focused and motivated as you see your scores improving. It will also help you to identify the areas you need to focus on.

SETTING GOALS

Once you have completed the assessment you can use it to set your goals for your new lifestyle. Goals are important, they give us something to work towards and they can keep us motivated and on the right track. However, sometimes they can have the opposite effect, so it's important you get these right.

1.   Set realistic goals – they need to be achievable and they need to suit your day-to-day life. If you're already struggling to fit in everything in your life, don't set a goal to run a marathon in six months, for example, especially if you're not even a runner (yet). When it comes to weight loss, you should not aim for any more than 2lbs per week and always give yourself a few easier weeks. For example, if you have 10lbs to lose, give yourself twelve weeks to lose this. If you reach your goal sooner, that's great, you're an overachiever and should be very proud of yourself. It's much better this way, rather than aiming to lose the weight in five weeks and feeling like a failure when you 'only' lose 5lbs in that time.

2.   Make goals measurable. Ideally you would go by how you feel rather than what the scales say, but this is not easily measured and being able to measure your progress is important if you ever want to achieve anything. So while you focus on how you feel and let that guide you to knowing what weight is right for you, you still need to weigh yourself to keep track of your progress.

3.   Break big goals into smaller steps. If you have 20–50lbs to lose to get to your healthy weight range, that can seem impossible. Break this into smaller sub-goals – take 5lbs at a time, even 2lbs. Or you might look for attainable goals, e.g. if you're currently 203lbs, then aim to get to under 200lbs first and then 195lbs and so on. Reaching each sub-goal will give you a confidence boost and before you know it, step by step, you've reached your target. And while you're en route to your big goal, do not look ahead and get down about how far you still have to go; look behind and feel proud of how

far you've come – every pound you've lost means you've done something right!

4.   Set goals other than just weight loss. Look at your self-check – where did you score badly? Eating sugar? Sleep quality? Fitness? Set goals around these – e.g. I want to improve my sleep quality score by 3 points in the next three weeks, or I want to exercise three times a week consistently for a month. All these goals go together, so when you start working on one, another area will benefit. When you start sleeping more, you'll have more energy to exercise, for example, and when you start exercising, your quality of sleep will improve.

5.   Allow some flexibility – you should be committed and focused but you should not be blindly fixated on your goals. Sometimes life happens. There might be a family crisis, a work crisis, a bereavement, illness or injury; these are times when you need to cut yourself some slack and accept that you might not make steady progress towards your goals. That's OK. When things get back to normal, you'll be ready to get back on track. It's worth noting, though, that you need to know when you should be going easy on yourself and when you're just making excuses and need to be tough on yourself.

6.   Don't have too many goals. Write down a list of your goals – everything you want to improve on. Then look at the list and see what you need to improve the most or what you want to start working on first. Pick a maximum of three – for example, lose 3lbs, improve my sleep quality score by 3 points and my think positive score by 4. Focus on these three first. Trying to do too many things at any one time never works.

The future – your weight-loss goal

Now that you have learned from your past and figured out where you are in the present, you can start looking to the future. This is the exciting bit!

In this programme, we use a two-tier method of setting target weights. First, the practical way, which is boring but necessary, as it helps us keep track easily, and being able to track your progress is important for motivation. So instead of finding your 'ideal' weight (who decides what's ideal for you, anyway?) we focus on your healthy weight range.

The chart overleaf shows a basic healthy weight range for women based on height, so the range given is fairly wide and where you should be within that range depends on your build. For example, if you're 5ft 4in your healthy weight can be anything between 7st 10lb and 10st 6lbs. Your first big target should be to get within this range. If you're a long way off, keep this as your long-term goal, something on the horizon that you know you're going to get to one day, you're just not exactly sure when. In the meantime, take it a few pounds at a time. Breaking your big goal into smaller ones is the only way to make it.

Other great ways of tracking your progress are checking your fat percentage and/or taking your measurements. Sometimes you might see progress in these before you see it on the scales. For checking your fat percentage you will need scales that measure this, or have it checked at the gym or at your doctor's. For taking your measurements, all you need is a measuring tape – once a week measure the circumference of your bust, waist, hips and thighs, making sure you always take your measurements at the exact same spots.

Healthy weight range chart:

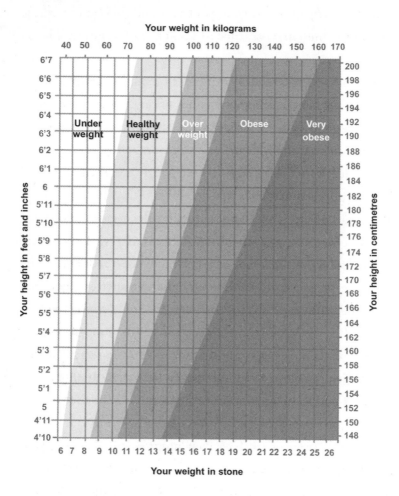

Find your happy weight

The second way of finding your goal weight, and the one I prefer, is finding your 'happy weight' – a weight that you feel happy with. When will you be happy with your weight and your body? The answer to this is not a number but a feeling – numbers (clothes size, weight) are someone else's opinion of what weight you should be; the way for YOU to decide when you're at the right weight for

YOU is to decide when you'll feel happy in your skin. Ultimately, you will only know this when you actually get there, but for now, you can imagine that situation. So sit down and ask yourself: *How will it feel to be happy with my weight? How will my life be different? How will I behave?* Write down all your answers, even the small details.

Some typical answers we get to this question are:

- When I can try on anything in a shop and not think, 'I look fat in this.'

- When I can wear a swimsuit in public and not feel self-conscious.

- When I don't think about my weight all day, every day.

- When I no longer feel the need to talk about my weight with my friends.

- When I no longer care what the latest diet is.

- When I smile all the time, move with confidence and ease, and my steps are light.

Visualise your happy weight

When you've written down what it will be like to be happy with your weight, focus on how you will *feel* – this is really important. Close your eyes, relax, take a deep breath and imagine yourself at your happy weight, the weight you've just described above. Imagine feeling happy with your weight; you love your body and you feel confident. *Feel* it in your heart, *really* feel it. Feel it as if you were at your target already. How does it feel? Doesn't it feel amazing? Spend 5 minutes really enjoying that great feeling with every cell of your being. What a wonderful feeling! This is your target weight. You want to feel this great all the time, don't you? You might have to work to get there but if you feel this great at the end, it'll be worth it. The great news is, you will start feeling great long before you get to your target! In fact, doing this visualisation daily will make you feel much happier with your body right now!

Do this exercise as often as you want, as it will help you stay really focused on your end goal and remind you that it's worth the effort. A good time to do this is first thing in the morning, as it will remind you of your goals and get you focused for the day. Whenever you're tempted to eat something unhealthy, remind yourself of the feeling and ask yourself, 'Do I want to get to a point where I feel this amazing about myself all the time or do I want this piece of cake? Which one do I want more?' Quite an easy choice isn't it? If you still find yourself going for the cake, you will need to work on your self-belief, which is something we'll talk about later in the book.

Plan how to reach your goals

Now you've set your goals, it's important to think how about you are actually going to reach them. There's no point in having goals unless you come up with some sort of plan to achieve them. This book will give you plenty of ideas, so don't worry, you don't have to come up with them by yourself, but what you will need to do yourself is track your goals.

Tracking is really important, as otherwise you will lose focus. I recommend you use a journal (or journal app) in which you write down all your goals and prioritise them. Pick your top three goals. Then write down your 'daily habits' – what is it that you have to do to reach these goals? What can you do every day? As your goals will be weight-loss related, all you have to do is follow the plan, but once you have this, you will have to prioritise and choose which changes you want to focus on from week to week. Once you've chosen your habits to focus on, keep track every day – how did you do today?

ACTIONS

1. Complete all the exercises in this chapter.

2. Resist the temptation to follow the latest fad diet.

3. Repeat the self-assessment regularly.

4. Set your goals and prioritise these.

5. Make sure you know your target healthy weight range.

6. Have your happy-weight vision firmly in your head. Get in the habit of visualising this every day.

2

THE ROOT OF THE PROBLEM – EMOTIONAL EATING

In this chapter you'll learn:

- If your relationship with food is healthy or unhealthy.
- The importance of self-respect.
- The key to overcoming emotional eating.
- The problem with women's magazines.

What is your relationship with food like? Have you ever thought about it? Do you love food, yet hate it? Maybe you hate the fact that it's making you gain weight? Does eating make you feel good? Do you eat to nourish your body or to nurture your heart? Why do you eat the things you eat?

Your relationship with food is the absolute key to weight-loss success. The fact is, the main reason behind women's weight issues is emotional eating – in other words, an unhealthy relationship with food; food is an emotional matter for us. Advertisers know this and so many food ads, especially ads for chocolate aimed at women, appeal to emotions. Don't be fooled by this! As long as your relationship with food is bad, as long as there are emotions involved, it will be hard to lose weight; you will need to use a lot of will-power. You can still lose weight, but it is going to be hard work and it's unlikely to be sustainable. It is essential to solve the root issue first – emotional eating – which will then make your weight-loss journey easy and exciting.

YOUR RELATIONSHIP WITH FOOD

How do you know if you have a bad relationship with food? These are some of the typical signs:

- You are an emotional eater – you eat when you're stressed, sad, lonely, angry or feel any other negative emotions. You think food will cheer you up and make you feel better.

- You are always on a diet and you go through periods of being super strict and not allowing yourself any 'treats'.

- You see food as a weight-management tool; everything you eat is either good or bad for weight loss.

- You often overeat, continuing to eat after you're full, to the point of feeling uncomfortable.

- You view many foods as forbidden (yet you often end up bingeing on these).

Further signs of emotional eating include sudden hunger, craving specific unhealthy foods (your crutches), urgent hunger that has to be satisfied right away, feeling hungry after a burst of strong emotions and feeling a sense of regret or guilt after eating. The guilt is a giveaway. When you have a healthy relationship with food, you don't eat that Mars bar because you need it to comfort you, you eat it because you want to eat it and that's it, you don't feel guilty after it. You enjoyed it and you move on, no regrets. When, however, you're eating it for emotional reasons, you feel crap afterwards, you beat yourself up about it, how you shouldn't have eaten it, how weak you are. This makes you feel down, and before you know it you're soothing your emotions with some more comfort food.

Emotional eating is a cycle you can get caught in. It is a very common problem and many people don't even realise it's a problem that can be fixed. Maybe you're not even aware that you're doing it, or you think that's just the way you are, you can't help it.

In contrast, if you have a healthy relationship with food:

- You enjoy food, mostly healthy foods, but sometimes some of the bad stuff too, and you never feel guilty for it!

- You eat when you are physically hungry.

- You eat a balanced and varied diet full of foods you like.

- You're rarely on a diet.

- You stop eating when you feel satisfied.

When you have a healthy relationship with food, you eat food that fuels your body, heals your body, gives you energy and supports your health (whereas, the foods we usually crave do the opposite – make you lethargic/zap your energy, make you sick and depressed). You don't need food when things go wrong, when you are bored or depressed. You don't need food to soothe your emotions or fill a void. You don't obsess about every mouthful you eat, or count calories, points, or feel the need to exercise every calorie off. You eat when you are hungry and stop when you are satisfied – you don't overeat to the point of being uncomfortable (except maybe at Christmas), you are also able to enjoy some treats without feeling guilty and one biscuit doesn't lead to the whole pack being gone within half an hour.

Do you identify with any of the negative behaviours above? It can be hard to admit that your relationship with food is unhealthy, that you're a big emotional eater. I understand this because I have been (and still am at times) the world's biggest emotional eater. It is a strange thing, because most of the women I meet are emotional eaters, yet we find it really hard to admit that we do it. Part of it is a sense of embarrassment – we don't want people to think we're pigs; it's disgusting.

The first step to take is to admit that this is me; I am an emotional eater. There's no need to be ashamed. It does not mean you're a weak person, no matter what people may lead you to believe. There are many people working in the weight-loss industry who just don't understand emotional eating: they tell you to be strong, to stop doing that to yourself. 'I just don't understand why anyone would eat this crap. Just get off your backside and stop eating crap; be strong. Take responsibility!' These are the kind of things you hear all the time and, yes, they are true, but if you're someone struggling with emotional eating (which I think most women struggle with to some extent), that tone is not going to work on you. Quite the opposite; it makes you feel like you're weak and useless. But you're not weak; you just have an issue you need to sort out and you will be able to overcome it. Being able to admit the problem to yourself (you do not need to announce it on Facebook) shows that you are strong, you're taking ownership of your problems and you're going to fix this thing once and for all, because it can be fixed, and once you've fixed it, you'll be a new person.

The fact is, food does *not* heal emotions or solve problems. It doesn't remove boredom or relieve depression; it doesn't make you less lonely or stressed. All it does is give you a momentary escape and then leave you feeling bad about yourself. For an escape with a more positive outcome read a good book or watch a movie!

The media loves to talk about food addiction these days. While it exists, in most cases it would be better described as emotional eating. Food in itself is not addictive – you might think you can't live without chocolate, for example, but really, you can. Telling ourselves 'I'm addicted' just gives us an excuse to continue doing what we're doing and also makes stopping seem unnecessarily hard.

Emotional eating is the root cause of weight issues for most women. Once you fix your relationship with food, you will become one of those people who seem to be able to eat anything and never gain weight! You'll be able to enjoy food and never need to diet again.

OVERCOMING EMOTIONAL EATING

For many, these problems run deep and they take time and effort to correct, sometimes even counselling, but you can start right now. The first thing is to recognise why you're overeating. Start keeping a food diary (for how to do this see p. 129) and write in it why you ate (physical hunger or a certain emotion) and your feelings at the time of eating. Another important thing to note is how you felt after eating. If you ate because you were angry, did the food take that anger away? How did you feel an hour later? Did the food solve your problem? Or did it possibly create another one (guilt)?

Once you've identified the situations where you do this, next time you're in the same situation you will be more aware of it and can stop and ask yourself, 'Do I really need the food and do I even want it?'

When you realise what is making you want to eat and that food doesn't solve any problems, indeed it often leaves you feeling worse, it will be easier to turn down that cake or refuse that biscuit, safe in the knowledge that you're doing it because you actually don't want it, rather than because you can't have it.

Table 1: Physical hunger v emotional hunger

Physical hunger	Emotional hunger
Builds up gradually and can wait	Comes on suddenly and feels urgent
Can be satisfied with any food	Can only be satisfied by specific (unhealthy) foods: pizza, crisps, chocolate, etc.
Allows you to stop eating once your hunger is satisfied	Causes you to overeat and feel uncomfortably full
Leaves you feeling satisfied after eating, never guilty	Leaves you feeling guilty and angry or disappointed with yourself after eating

Eating is a way of hiding from our problems and issues. I only realised this through my own experience in the last year when I went through some very challenging times, including separating from my husband. I was extremely busy, always looking after others' needs first (which is another thing most of us women have to stop doing) and then when I had time for myself I was too tired to do anything but collapse on the couch and eat something. I absolutely *had* to eat something. It was only when everything became too much and I actually had to face myself that I realised that the reason why I felt I *had* to eat was because I did not want to face all the messed-up emotions inside me.

After my separation I felt every difficult emotion you can feel: I was scared, hurt, stressed, angry, but most of all really overwhelmed. So I ate. It's as if you eat to stuff the problems and feelings deeper down. You need to keep shovelling food in because otherwise all the big scary feelings will claw their way out and you'll actually have to face them – and who wants to do that? Not me! The problem is that no matter how much you stuff them down, they aren't going anywhere and you then have the additional feelings of self-disgust and self-hatred to deal with.

In fact, I discovered that the only way to get rid of those emotions is to let them out. Stop trying to push them deeper down and face them. It will be very painful for a bit, but once you face them, they'll go away. In some cases you may have to face them many times, but eventually they will go away. So if you are caught in the cycle of emotional eating, the best thing to do, when you next feel like reaching for that bag of crisps, is to ask yourself, 'What is it that I'm really feeling? What feelings am I trying to hide?' Tell yourself that you are brave and strong enough to face them. Sit in silence. Let it all come out. Do not be afraid to feel your feelings, even the scarier ones like hurt and anger, because as long as you're eating to soothe them, you'll never be able to get rid of them.

THE KEY – SELF-RESPECT

At the root of many people's bad relationship with food lies a lack of self-respect, a lack of love for ourselves, self-hatred and a lack of self-acceptance. Some people punish themselves by eating all the wrong things. The belief that 'I don't deserve to be slim and happy with my body' keeps people overeating. Some people want to stay (in their opinion) unattractive so as not to attract attention; they hide behind all the weight.

It is surprising how many women do not love and respect themselves enough. We might think we do, but if you *really* loved and respected yourself, would you fill yourself with all those foods that you know are bad for you? That you know are going to make you gain weight, put you at risk of all sorts of diseases and make you cranky? Would you feed your kids those foods?

Food is fuel. Why do we stuff our bodies with foods that have the opposite effect? Instead of energising and fuelling us, they make us lethargic, slow and sick. Is that the way you show respect to your body? I am not saying that if you eat anything unhealthy you don't love yourself; of course you can have the odd treat – we all deserve that. But if day after day you stuff your face with unhealthy junk food that you know is no good for you and at the same time you'd love nothing more than to be slim, then chances are you don't really respect yourself.

How to learn to love yourself

Learning to really love and respect yourself is a process that takes some time, but the great thing is that as soon as you start working on it, you will start feeling the changes in your life almost immediately. Here are some ways to show you that you love yourself.

1. Put your own needs first

I have started with probably the most challenging thing. Women have this great need to please others, keep everyone else happy and ignore themselves. Putting your own needs first is often seen as selfish. But you need to understand that looking after yourself, making yourself happy first, is not selfish. It's a cliché, but it's true, that if you make sure you're happy and well looked after, then you'll be much better able to look after others. It is important to learn to say, 'No, actually I can't do that right now.' I know it's hard but once you learn to do it, you'll actually learn to love it and you will respect yourself so much more.

2. Make time for yourself – treat yourself

Do something nice for yourself regularly. This can be whatever you enjoy – a facial, getting your nails done, a lie in, going for a walk or a run, buying new shoes, going to the beach alone or having a pamper evening at home alone. Whatever it is, make sure it's something relaxing and special that makes you feel good about yourself.

3. Accept yourself the way you are

This is unconditional love. You love your family, your kids, your friends without any conditions, don't you? Or do you say, 'I would love you, if only you could be a bit slimmer, a bit more successful, a bit less annoying, etc.'? I didn't think so. Yet we say these things to ourselves. We're never good enough for ourselves. To truly move forward, to get that body you've always wanted, you need to learn to accept what you have today. Once you learn to love the body you have, no matter what size it is, you will naturally want to treat it with more respect and eat healthily, which means you will lose weight and it'll be relatively easy. You are what you are; no one is perfect (what is perfect, anyway?) so stop being so hard on yourself. From now on, only say nice things to yourself and remember, if you don't have anything nice to say, don't say anything.

4. Write down five positive things about yourself every day

This is a great exercise to do, particularly if you tend to be really hard on yourself. Every evening, write down five positive things about yourself: things you did well, things you like about yourself;

they can be anything as long as they're positive reasons to love yourself today.

5. Look after yourself

The best way to show you love yourself is to treat yourself with the respect you deserve. Look after yourself by nourishing your body with good, nutritious food, and be active, exercise. This is obviously hard to do when you're dealing with your emotional eating issues and only starting to build self-respect, but as you make progress it'll become easier, and managing to treat yourself well will make you respect yourself even more. Remember that fast-fix crash diets are not a very respectful way to treat yourself! It is not about the weight, it's about nourishing yourself, keeping your body healthy and strong – that is how you show yourself respect, regardless of your weight.

There are loads of books and websites on this subject, so if it's something you feel you really need to work on, it helps to read up on it. If you feel that your self-esteem is really low and you find it hard to do anything about it, you might want to consider talking to a therapist.

TAKING CONTROL OF EMOTIONAL EATING

While you're working on getting to the root of the problem and facing your emotions, here are some practical tips for managing emotional eating:

1. Use your food diary to identify your different triggers. Is it stress at work? Boredom? Anger? Do you need it to relax in the evenings? Fear? Loneliness? Is it to avoid your feelings?

2. Once you've identified your trigger situations, ask yourself, 'How did eating help me in this situation? How did I feel while eating? Did it help me or did it make things worse?' Most likely, you will find that eating a chocolate bar, or whatever is your go-to comfort food, does not help the situation. It might give you a temporary escape or relief, but very soon afterwards you will feel bad – you might feel physically unwell or hate yourself for yet again ruining your diet, so in the end, it only adds to your problems.

3. Now think, 'Could I have dealt with the situation differently?' Most likely the answer is yes. Here are some suggestions for what you can do in a situation like this:

    - Go for a walk.

    - Come up with things to say to yourself to talk yourself out of it, to remind yourself that food is not the answer, that it's not going to solve anything; in fact, it's likely to make things worse.

    - Go and brush your teeth; having that fresh and minty feeling in your mouth can reduce the desire to eat.

    - Write about how you feel. Let it all out, release the emotions so there's nothing food needs to soothe any more.

    - Do something productive for 30 minutes and see if you still feel the same (this will buy you some time and hopefully the urge will pass).

    - If you really feel like you have to have that chocolate, try having one square and really savour and enjoy the taste. You may find this is enough to satisfy you when you actually pay attention to what you are eating. Often when we eat as a result of emotional cues, we devour the food within minutes without paying any attention to the taste and sensations, and are left still feeling unsatisfied.

4.   In your diary, note the times you manage to avoid emotional eating and how you feel after this (you should feel great!). Compare this to the times you binge, so in the future you can contrast these two outcomes in your mind – you have a choice.

5.   When you successfully resist the urge to binge, make a point of being *really* proud of yourself and notice how you feel: Did you need the food? Was it really that hard to resist? This will boost your confidence, and next time it'll be much easier to resist the urge. Quite often, you just need to break the cycle.

6.   Ask yourself, 'On a scale of 1–10 how hungry am I?' Establish if you are suffering from head hunger (emotional cues) or stomach hunger (genuine physical need for food). Are you really hungry or merely responding to something else that has happened? Have a glass of water or a cup of herbal tea to distract yourself and to allow the desire to subside if it is a case of head hunger.

7.   Reduce the temptations in the house; if you know you comfort eat biscuits, don't keep them in the house. Instead have some healthy snacks available.

8.   When you do give in to the temptation, do not feel guilty. Guilt will only lead to lower self-esteem, and consequently it will become harder to handle the situation next time. Analyse it, put it behind you and move on. No guilt. Remember also

that someone with a healthy relationship with food is able to enjoy a little bit of the bad stuff without feeling guilty – you don't need to be a saint and you don't need to use strong will-power. You need to make peace with food.

9. Further to the above two points: do not see food as the enemy or as the solution to all your problems. Take the emotion out of food and remember that one bar of chocolate will not lead to you piling on the pounds. A lapse is very different to a relapse; do not let eating that one chocolate bar lead to devouring the contents of your cupboards and calling the local takeaway. A lapse will not have a big impact on your weight loss, but a relapse may. Do not write your whole day off because of one small indiscretion.

10. Accept yourself the way you are. Making any changes in life starts with accepting and loving yourself the way you are right now, right here. Stop being so hard on yourself, feeling like you're never good enough. Focus on the positive in yourself and you will start seeing positive changes.

11. See food as fuel and junk food as just that – junk. How can something that makes you feel sick really be a treat? If you want to treat your body, give it something really healthy! Or treat yourself with non-food-related luxuries – take time out to paint your nails, read a chapter of your book, phone a friend for a catch-up, etc.

Here's a great real-life example from one of my clients, Ruth, who was really unhappy in her job. Her boss was difficult so she comfort ate her way through the day at work, which led to her gaining

2 stone and hating not only her boss but herself as well. This is a typical situation from her food diary:

3 p.m.: muffin

Reason: *My boss was rude to me again; I was upset and annoyed (I hate her!).*

Thoughts while eating: *Argh! I hate that b****! I need to get out of here!*

Outcome: *I relaxed a bit while eating though I hardly noticed I had eaten the whole muffin because I was so busy fuming!*

1 hour later: *I'm annoyed with myself for eating that muffin. I can't believe I've done it again. I was doing so well with my diet and now I've done this. I always do this. Why can't I just learn? My boss is still a cow. I hate her and now I hate myself.*

Analysis: In hindsight, Ruth realised that eating the muffin didn't help the situation; it actually made it worse because now not only does Ruth hate her boss, she hates herself as well. More importantly, she is taking her anger at her boss out on herself and she is only hurting herself with this – her boss is none the wiser. Looking at it this way was a real eye-opener for Ruth, as she was able to see how pointless her actions were and how they made her more unhappy.

The solution: Ruth started going for long walks at lunchtime to clear her head, improve her mood, get some exercise and keep her away from junk food (lunchtime was another time when she tended to binge eat). This made her feel great about herself – she was doing something good for herself and she was in control of the situation. Getting out of the office also gave her a break from the pressure and so helped her cope better in the afternoons. While it didn't make her boss any nicer, it made Ruth better able to deal with the situation. Whenever there was a situation that made her want to binge, she first removed herself from the situation by going to the toilet or going to get some water – anything to get her away and give her a few extra minutes to take a deep breath and remind herself how pointless bingeing on chocolate and cakes was.

Once she had looked at the situation objectively like this, it was actually relatively easy for her to make the changes, and every time she managed to get through one situation without bingeing, her confidence was boosted, which made dealing with difficult situations easier.

It is really important to keep in mind that food is fuel; it is meant to nourish, not nurture. Just remembering this can make a huge difference to people's lives and their relationship with food. Another thing that will really help you is learning to understand nutrition and, in particular, how junk food affects us, so please read the section on sugar and processed food in chapter 4 carefully.

ONE MORE THING: THE MEDIA

Women's magazines, the gossipy kind, are one of my pet peeves. Don't get me wrong, there are some good magazines out there, but they do seem to be in the minority these days. The main problem with these magazines is that they send contradictory messages. For example, on page 5: 'OMG *look at Victoria Beckham, she's lost weight again*' (if she actually lost weight every time the magazine headlines claimed she had, she would have disappeared by now) and, '*This celeb is far too skinny. Look at her body, yuck, disgusting!*' On page 6, '*So and so put on weight again, not looking good*'; page 8

'I'm proud of my curves' (curvy now being synonymous with being overweight, rather than actually having a curvy figure); page 10 *'how to get a model body in just 3 weeks with our easy to follow eat nothing diet'*; page 14 *'how to bake the best ever cupcakes'* and so on. Do you see how contradictory the messages are? So many women read these magazines and they feel confused and irritated. What am I meant to be: skinny, fat or curvy?

It is easy for me to sit here and say not to let anyone tell you what you should and shouldn't be – that is for you to decide and no one else should have any say in that, as long as you're happy with yourself. But let's face it, most people these days are not immune to peer pressure and these magazines can have a huge influence on people's lives. If you read them, of course you are going to be confused – I see this all the time with clients and my first advice is always to stop reading them. Take a month not reading *any* magazines, gossip sites etc., unfollow them on social media, and see the difference it makes. Even a week is a good start. People tell me all the time how much better they feel after they stop reading the magazines, so try it for yourself!

EXERCISES TO HELP STOP EMOTIONAL EATING

These exercises can really help with overcoming emotional eating and improving your relationship with food:

1. When you want to binge:

Ask yourself:

- What is it that I really need? Is it food or something else?

- Will food help me get what I want?

- If I do eat this [insert food you're about to binge on] how will I feel afterwards? How will I feel about it tomorrow? Will I regret it?

- If I don't eat it, how will I feel? How will I feel tomorrow?

- If, for the next four weeks/three months/six months, I stop these binges, how will I feel? How will I look?

Then create an image in your head of yourself looking healthy, slim and carefree – like someone who eats healthily and is happy with their body and diet.

2. When you've just had a binge:

Ask yourself:

- Was it worth it?

- How do I feel?

- Has it fixed the problem?

3. When you've managed to resist your urge to binge:

Ask yourself:

- How do I feel?

- Has the problem been fixed?

- Would food have made it better/easier?

- How would I feel had I given in to the urge?

- Was it hard to resist the urge? Is it getting easier?

It is important to do these exercises as they help you learn from the situation and make you better able to manage similar situations in the future.

It is worth writing in a journal or your food diary all your observations. Learning to understand your behaviour is the first step to making changes and it will also make these changes far easier to make.

ACTIONS

1. Do everything you can to overcome your unhealthy relationship with food.

2. Start treating yourself with love and respect.

3. Avoid all gossip magazines!

3

NUTRITION MADE SIMPLE – BACK TO BASICS

In this chapter you'll learn:

- How to fuel your body.

- What a balanced diet is.

- Why carbohydrates are important.

- Why fat is good for weight loss.

- The importance of water.

Science is not my strong point, so a big thanks to Slim with Tina nutritionist Elaine for helping me with this section.

Most diets tell you to eat this, don't eat that, without really telling you the reason why. Even worse are the diets that tell you to eat something and not eat something else simply because it helps you lose weight faster (e.g. high-protein/no-carbs diets) without any regard to the impact on your long-term overall health. Some diets do educate you, but only in (fast) weight loss rather than health (though they might call this nutrition and make it sound as if it is healthy). You never question this because the diet has been developed by some expert or another and it's probably backed up by scientific research (isn't everything?). And it's probably true – you will lose weight, but as we've already established, it's not going to last and there's a good chance it's not going to be very healthy either.

In my opinion, it is essential that you learn to understand enough about nutrition to know what is good for you and what isn't good for you from a *health* point of view, rather than a weight-loss angle – a healthy, balanced diet, free of any junk, is going to lead to weight loss. This is a fact, so there's no need to focus on weight loss only. It is also important to understand the role of certain nutrients, for example why you need carbohydrates and why the right kinds of fats are essential. This chapter will help you understand how to fuel your body properly.

FAT LOSS VERSUS WEIGHT LOSS

On quick fix diets you can lose a huge amount of weight in just a week or two, but what the scales are reflecting is a loss of mainly water weight, perhaps a small amount of actual fat loss and, in some cases, a loss of muscle mass caused by dramatic calorie restriction.

When you are looking to reduce your body size you want to focus on fat loss, maintaining your lean muscle mass. A rate of 1–2lbs per week is healthy and ensures that the loss you see is from fat and not just water weight, or even worse, lean muscle. It is vital that you maintain your lean muscle, as the more muscle you have the greater your metabolic rate will be. The key to maintaining muscle mass is eating enough and taking in enough protein so that your body doesn't have to resort to its muscle mass for energy. Regular resistance training is beneficial for maintaining and building upon your existing muscle.

FOOD IS FUEL

The first thing you need to do is to start seeing food as fuel. The ultimate reason you should eat is to fuel your body, to provide your cells with all the nutrients they need to keep you strong and healthy. Yet how often do you actually think of food in this way?

We tend to value food for its taste, or even the way it looks, rather than its nutritional value. We eat with our eyes. Think about TV shows like *MasterChef* – everything has to look amazing and all the judges talk about is the taste – they can go on for minutes getting very excited and using rich language to describe the texture and flavour of the food. This is the opposite of how we should make our food choices. Food is meant to nourish our bodies, not just please our eyes or soothe our emotions. I know you probably think that healthy food is terribly boring, but this is not true and hopefully the recipes and tips provided in this book will prove that to you.

If you have kids, start talking to them about food as fuel rather than choosing foods based on taste – how 'yummy' something is. It can, and will, still be yummy and there can be the odd treat, but talk to them about how this fish is going to help their muscles grow strong so that they can play sports, for example. This will help them develop a healthy attitude towards food and educate them so they won't have to struggle with weight and their relationship with food in the future.

Doing something like changing your dietary habits as a family is a great way to bond and I've noticed that those who get their kids and/or partners, or their flatmates involved are more likely to succeed – probably because they see it not just as another weight-loss plan but a healthy lifestyle change.

Have you ever looked at a food item and wondered if it will give you energy? Probably not, and don't feel bad if you haven't, because not many people actually do this – we are far more concerned with 'Does this make me fat?' or 'How does this taste? Will it make me feel good?' Next time you pick something up, ask yourself, 'How is this going to fuel me?' If the answer is, 'In no way; in fact, it'll probably make me feel lethargic, make me bloated and possibly affect my skin,' then don't eat it. Or if you do eat it, at least you are aware of the fact that you're eating junk – sometimes this is OK; don't beat yourself up about it. Allowing yourself a little bit of chocolate every now and then can actually prevent you from bingeing on a family-size bar after denying yourself for weeks, and being able to do this without feeling any guilt shows that you have a healthy relationship with food.

A BALANCED DIET

A balanced diet is the key to health. I have to be clear, though, because often when people (dieters) say things like, 'It's all about balance' or 'I aim to eat a balanced diet,' they mean a diet that includes a good dose of the bad stuff. This is not the kind of balance I'm talking about! A balanced diet means that you include each food group in the right proportion in your diet – protein, fats and carbohydrates – you do not cut out complete food groups or eat another in excess. And within these food groups you focus on the healthy ones, such as healthy carbs (as you'll learn soon, a lot of carbs are not good for you; see table 2 overleaf for examples). Treats of the rubbishy kind shouldn't be a permanent feature in a balanced diet.

When you want to lose weight, you should limit your carbohydrate intake to the lower end of the scale and increase your protein and fat intake slightly. There is no need to go any lower than 45 per cent on carbohydrates as long as you eat the right ones – eating the wrong carbs is often the problem. This can be hard for people to believe, but trust me, give it a try. In fact, many times I've seen girls on our plan say they'd been avoiding carbs for a long time and only when they added them back in did they actually start making progress on weight loss.

Table 2: Components of a balanced diet

	Why you need it	Where to best get it	What to limit
Protein (10–25% of your diet)	Growth, tissue repair, immune function, making of essential hormones	Fish, poultry, nuts, seeds	Red meat, cheese
Carbohydrates (45–65% of your diet)	Energy source, provides fibre	Fruit, vegetables, whole grains such as oats, quinoa, buckwheat and millet, and sweet potato	White bread, rice, pasta, etc., biscuits and confectionary, processed foods
Fats (20–35% of your diet)	Energy source, for absorbing certain vitamins, formation of cell membranes	Olive oil, coconut oil, nuts, seeds, oily fish, avocado	Cakes, biscuits, fried foods, takeaways, processed foods

It is important to note that the above chart is for the general population and there can be individual differences depending on age, activity levels and other factors, but this is good to have as a basis to get you started.

Don't get too hung up on the percentages above. You do not need to start measuring and weighing things. The easiest way to ensure that you get enough of everything is to make sure that you have both carbs and protein in every meal – including your snacks – and add some good oils in wherever you can.

A healthy dinner plate:

• Vegetables should take up half your plate.

• Lean protein should fill one-quarter.

• Starchy carbs/grains/legumes should take up the last quarter.

CARBOHYDRATES

Carbohydrates have been given a bad name by numerous popular diets such as Atkins and Dukan, all of which advocate cutting out most, if not all, carbohydrates. While there are some carbohydrates that are bad for you, not all should be tarred with the same brush – it's important to make the distinction between good and bad carbs.

Good carbohydrates are an essential part of a healthy diet. They provide some vital nutrients, such as B vitamins and various minerals, as well as being a source of energy for the body, all of which are essential for optimal health. They also provide a source of fibre, which is necessary for a fully functioning digestive system and for preventing constipation (it's no wonder that many high-protein/no-carb diets recommend you take a fibre supplement).

What are carbs?

Put simply, carbohydrates are composed of one or more simple sugar molecules. Once digested, all carbs (regardless of the source) are broken down into glucose, which is then circulated in your blood to be used as energy by the cells of the body. Glucose is the preferred fuel of the brain, muscles and nervous system – in other words, carbs are important for the functioning of your brain and nervous system. This is why people often feel irritable and foggy-headed when they initially cut carbs out of their diet when trying out the latest low- or no-carb diet.

When glucose enters the bloodstream, your pancreas releases insulin in response. The role of insulin is to maintain blood sugar levels and keep them within certain ranges. Insulin moves glucose from the blood to the cells of the body, where it is used for energy. Anything that is not used for immediate energy needs will be stored in the liver or the muscles in the form of glycogen. After the liver and muscle stores have been saturated, any remaining glucose will be converted and stored as fat. When there is too much glucose in your blood (from eating too many or the wrong type of carbs) your body has to release more insulin. Your liver and muscles can only hold a small amount of glucose at any one time, but the insulin still has all that glucose to get rid of and the only place left is the fat-storage cells. This is why it is important that you do not overconsume carbs (which is what many people tend to do!).

Simple carbs – the bad carbs!

Simple sugars are for the most part found in foods which have been processed and hence stripped of all nutritional value and fibre content. These are often referred to as empty calories because they offer no nutritional benefits. They are made up of short chains of sugar molecules, which are digested rapidly into glucose and hence provide a readily available short burst of energy.

Carbs containing simple sugars often encourage people to over-eat and consequently lead to weight gain. They are all too often combined with fat and additives into high-calorie foods such as cakes and biscuits. Simple carbs tend to be what people want when they comfort eat and it is easy to binge on them. Furthermore, they cause surges in blood sugar levels, resulting in insulin production, which in turn encourages fat storage, as described above. These are the bad guys that are behind most weight issues and hence give all carbs a bad name.

Not all simple carbs are bad, however. Wholefoods such as fruit and milk also contain naturally occurring simple sugars, fructose and lactose, but these are much healthier than the sugars in processed foods due to the presence of vitamins, minerals and fibre. Sucrose, which is table sugar, is what you really need to reduce and avoid, as well as all products that contain it.

What are wholefoods?

Wholefoods are foods which exist in their natural state and remain, for the most part, unprocessed and unrefined and contain no additives such as sugar, salt, preservatives, etc.

Complex and fibrous carbohydrates – the good carbs

Complex carbohydrates are made up of complex chains of sugar molecules which take longer to digest and therefore are broken down more slowly, providing a slower, steady supply of energy. This limits the amount of sugar stored as fat. These are carbohydrates that are mostly unprocessed and unrefined, and which occur naturally. Good examples of complex carbohydrates include oats, spelt, legumes, sweet potato, beans, brown rice and vegetables. Vegetables are fibrous complex carbs and are an invaluable low-calorie source of nutrients and fibre.

Complex carbohydrates are a vital source of many essential vitamins and minerals, such as vitamins A and C, the B vitamins, magnesium, iron and calcium to name but a few, as well as providing a great source of fibre.

Wholegrains v refined grains

Wholegrains supply an abundant source of nutrients associated with reducing your risk of diseases such as heart disease and bowel cancer. When grains are processed (or 'refined') to make them look whiter, the part of the grain that contains fibre and many useful nutrients is removed. This means that white bread, pasta and cereals are not beneficial to your health at all; in fact they are bad for you. Wholegrains are also more likely to keep you feeling fuller for longer, as they generally contain more fibre and take longer to digest than foods that have been processed. This can help to control your appetite, while also assisting in weight loss and maintenance.

Fibre

Fibre is the indigestible part of the food which we eat and is a vital component of our diet. It is only found in plant foods and is made up of two main types – soluble and insoluble fibre. Diets low in fibre have been associated with constipation, haemorrhoids and an increased risk of cancers such as colon cancer. A diet rich in fibre on the other hand has been shown to lead to a reduced risk of cardiovascular disease and obesity, while helping to maintain normal blood sugar levels and reduce blood cholesterol.

Fibre slows down the digestive system, resulting in a longer digestion period and increasing satiety. This creates a steady release of glucose into the bloodstream and a slower release of insulin, resulting in a long-lasting, steady flow of energy that won't have you crashing at 3 p.m. in the afternoon.

Dietary fibre is essential for a healthy and fully functioning digestive system; both types have health benefits. **Soluble fibre**, found in beans, vegetables, oats, fruit and rye, slows the digestion of food, resulting in a controlled rise in blood sugar. It can also help lower cholesterol. **Insoluble fibre** cannot dissolve in water and passes quickly through the digestive system, lowering the risk of constipation and reducing the risk of heart disease. Insoluble fibre, which is also known as roughage, can be found in oats, lentils, pulses and wholegrain bread, cereal, pasta and rice.

You should increase your fibre intake gradually and ensure you are drinking adequate fluids at the same time. Drastically increasing your fibre intake can put a strain on your digestive system and lead to some undesirable effects. It is recommended that the average adult has a daily intake of between 24g and 35g of fibre. Currently almost 80 per cent of Irish adults do not meet this recommendation.

THE GOOD – EAT THESE	THE BAD – AVOID THESE
Wholegrain bread	White bread
Wholegrain pasta	White pasta
Wholegrain rice	White rice
Spelt	Pastries, cakes, biscuits
Buckwheat	Sweets
Barley	Processed juices and other drinks
Rye	Sugar, including dextrose, sucrose, glucose, fructose, maltose, fruit syrup and fructose syrup
Millet	
Oats	
Vegetables	
Fruit	
Quinoa	
Sweet potato	
Buckwheat	
Polenta	

Carbs that I love are quinoa, oats, spelt bread, spelt pasta, brown rice, rice noodles, oatcakes and sweet potato.

Your face tells it all

Do you ever look in the mirror and your face looks kind of swollen or puffy? Some people call this a carb face and I think it's a pretty accurate description. I get a carb face if I eat anything from the bad list. It might not be obvious to others, but I notice it immediately. My face just fills up and my cheek bones seem to disappear. When I leave the bad stuff out again, within three days my face slims down a bit, the puffiness is gone and I can see my cheekbones again. Have you noticed this? If not, try leaving the bad stuff out for three days and see the difference!

Tina's Top Tips for controlling your carb intake:

1. When choosing carbohydrate foods always opt for fruit, fibrous vegetables and wholegrains high in fibre.

2. Avoid white foods – swap any white bread, pasta or rice for the wholegrain variety.

3. Avoid sugary treats and convenience foods such as pizza, chips, cakes and pastries.

4. Aim to get all your sugar from natural sources.

5. Swap sugary drinks for water or herbal teas.

6. Do not add sugar to hot drinks.

7. Buy sugar-free or naturally sweetened varieties of jam and marmalade.

8. Learn to read food labels – this is a key skill!

FAT

Fat is a vital and much needed macronutrient. Contrary to popular belief, fat should never be avoided if you are trying to reduce your body fat, so leaving out all the fat-free products should be one of the first things you do. In reality consuming the right kinds of fat can actually increase fat burning and subsequent weight loss. So the good news is, fat does not make you fat, quite the opposite. Sugar and not fat, as has been believed for years, is more than likely the reason you are reading this book and looking to transform your life. You just need to know the right fats to choose and those to avoid.

Why is fat important?

- It regulates body temperature.

- It supports the immune system.

- It's a source of energy.

- It maintains healthy cell function.

- It provides insulation and protection of vital body organs, including your brain.

- Vitamins A, D, E and K are all fat-soluble, which means that, for them to absorbed by the body, fat is needed.

Different types of fats – the good, the (not so) bad and the ugly

There are different types of fat, which come from different sources, and it is important that you understand the difference and know which type of fat you should be avoiding.

Good fats

Both polyunsaturated and monounsaturated fats are good fats, so you want these to be the fats you eat mostly.

Monounsaturated fats can be found in things like olive oil, avocado, nuts and olives. Monounsaturated fats have been linked with lowering cholesterol and reducing blood pressure, therefore promoting heart health. The Mediterranean diet is rich in mono-unsaturated fats and has been associated with some of the lowest rates of heart disease in the world.

Polyunsaturated fats can be found in fish, seafood, flaxseed and vegetable oils. There are two main types of polyunsaturated fats – omega 3 and omega 6 fatty acids. These are referred to as essential fatty acids, as our bodies are unable to create them and it is vital we consume them in our diet.

To promote optimal health it is important to have the correct balance when it comes to intake of omega 3 and 6 – an imbalance can lead to undesirable health effects. Omega 3 fatty acids are anti-inflammatory while omega 6 fatty acids are pro-inflamma-tory, and as our intake of omega 6 is usually much greater, this can lead to inflammation in the body, which in turn can lead to various health issues such as arthritis, heart disease, allergies and even cancer.

The majority of us eat far too much omega 6 and not enough omega 3. In fact, the only people in the world who are thought to eat these in the right proportions are the Japanese. Most of us just do not have enough sources of omega 3 in our diet. In contrast omega 6 oils are largely inexpensive and commonly used by food industries in the manufacture of many products such as cakes, biscuits and processed and convenience foods. Omega 3 fatty acids have been associated with protection against heart disease and a reduction in the symptoms of conditions like arthritis and eczema, so it's important to get enough of them.

Monounsaturated fats	Polyunsaturated fats, omega 3	Polyunsaturated fats, omega 6
Olive oil	Fish	Corn oil
Avocado	Flaxseed	Safflower oil
Rapeseed oil	Walnuts	Sunflower oil
Olives	Fish oils	
Nuts	Chia seeds	

Tina's Top Tips for reducing your omega 6 intake:

1. Limit your use of vegetable oils such as sunflower oil and corn oil.

2. Limit your intake of food products which are made using these oils.

3. Generally reduce your intake of processed and convenience foods and eat a diet of more natural and unprocessed foods.

Tina's Top Tips for adding omega 3 to your diet:

1. Oily fish is the best source – salmon (wild is better than farmed), mackerel, sardines, tuna.

2. Flaxseed, flaxseed oil and chia seed also provide omega 3.

3. Take a good quality omega 3 supplement.

The (not completely) bad – saturated fats

Saturated fats in the past have been linked with increased cholesterol and cardiovascular disease. However, this research is now disputed and it is understood that we can consume saturated fats in small amounts. Saturated fat actually has some important roles in the body, such as the formation of hormones and maintenance of cell membranes. Saturated fat is found in animal products such as dairy and red meat. It is also found in fried foods, confectionary, chocolate, cream, biscuits, cakes, pastries, etc. While it may be beneficial to watch your intake of the former, the main sources to focus on are the latter, as in addition to high levels of saturated fat, they contain high levels of sugar and little beneficial nutrition, whereas meat and dairy provide a source of vitamins and minerals which can be utilised by the body.

The ugly – trans fats

Trans fats are the worst fats of all and this is the one type of fat you should avoid at all costs. They have in fact been banned in many countries and are slowly being used less and less by the food industry. Trans fats are commonly found in processed foods, such as pastries, pizzas, margarine and baked goods. Trans fats can also hide under the names hydrogenated vegetable oil, partially hydrogenated oil, vegetable shortening and margarine, so look out for these on ingredients listings. Trans fats are known to raise bad cholesterol and cause cardiovascular disease.

The key with fats is to find a balance with the amount and types you consume. The main thing is not to cut out fat, but rather to choose fresh, natural, healthy sources such as nuts, seeds, oils, fish and avocado, to have saturated fats in small amounts and to reduce the amount of fat consumed from highly processed convenience food, such as biscuits, cakes, fast food, etc., which offer little in terms of nourishment.

How fats help you lose weight

Good fats, from things like avocado, nuts, seeds, olive oil, etc., slow down the emptying of the stomach after eating a meal, which results in a feeling of fullness and satiety for longer and reduces the temptation to rummage in the biscuit tin half an hour after eating. Try having some eggs and avocado for your breakfast one day and the next day have some cereal and low-fat milk and you'll see the difference for yourself!

As fat slows down digestion, it also slows the release of sugar into the blood stream, which helps with stabilising blood sugar levels. Steady blood sugar levels produce a steady stream of energy and keep hunger and food cravings at bay. This also means that your body does not have to release large amounts of insulin, resulting in reduced fat storage.

When you consume healthy fats you actually help your body to burn fat. Low-fat diets, in contrast, cause your body to hold on to all its fat stores as it senses fat is in low supply. So when you regularly eat (good) fat your body will start to use some of its stores for energy and other bodily needs.

Tina's Top Tips for eating the right fats:

1. Never choose low-fat products.

2. Always have a source of fat with salad, e.g. avocado, a boiled egg, a drizzle of olive oil.

3. The best oil for cooking is coconut oil.

4.   Eat oily fish twice a week.

5.   Snack on nuts and seeds.

Fats I love are olive oil, coconut oil, sesame oil, avocado, salmon and flaxseed.

PROTEIN

Protein is the building block of life due to the role it plays in the growth and repair of the body. Almost every cell and tissue in the body contains protein, so its inclusion in your diet is essential. Protein also plays a key role in the formation and function of cell membranes, hormones and enzymes. Proteins are made up of amino acids. When protein is digested it is broken down into these amino acids, which are then used by all the cells of the body (such as muscle, skin and hair) for growth, repair and maintenance.

Animal sources of protein	Plant sources of protein
Chicken	Soya beans
Turkey	Chickpeas
Beef	Lentils and other legumes
Fish	Beans
Eggs	Nuts, esp. almonds, walnuts
Cottage cheese	and hazelnuts
Buffalo mozzarella	Seeds
Yoghurt (natural and Greek	Quinoa
yoghurt)	Tofu
	Spirulina

There are two types of amino acids – **non-essential amino acids** (these can be made in the body) and **essential amino acids** (these cannot be made in the body and must be obtained from the diet). If a food contains all the essential amino acids it is said to be a **complete protein**. Examples of complete proteins include meat, fish, eggs and quinoa.

Why protein is so important for weight loss

Protein takes longer to digest than fat or carbohydrates; in other words, it moves through your body more slowly, which helps you feel fuller for longer. If you're one of those people who always feels hungry, you might not be eating enough protein at every meal. Breakfast is when people often miss out protein, opting for refined carbs instead, and then they're starving by 10 a.m. Digesting protein uses up more energy (calories) than digesting carbs or fat, which obviously is great for weight loss. Protein also helps maintain and build muscle mass, and the more muscles you have the greater your resting metabolism, i.e. those with more muscles will burn more calories at rest than those with no muscles. This is why some resistance training (such as weight training) is also great for weight loss.

When you want to lose weight, it's good to increase your protein intake a bit (but not excessively), but rather than getting caught up in the number of calories you're consuming, focus instead on including a protein source with every meal you eat – including your snacks.

My favourite protein foods are eggs, chickpeas, lentils, quinoa, black beans, almond butter, hummus, buffalo mozzarella, organic chicken, turkey and salmon.

WATER

Water is not only great for aiding weight loss but it is also vital for health – you can survive for two weeks without food but only days without water. Approximately two-thirds of your body is made up of water. Water is essential to our existence, assisting with all bodily functions and processes; every cell in the body requires water for optimal performance. It is consistently lost from the body on a daily basis via perspiration, tears, urine, breathing and exercise, so it is essential to constantly replenish your hydration levels. Water controls your body temperature, assists with weight control, gives you energy, transports nutrients, transports waste products, assists in digestion and absorption of food, prevents constipation, lubricates joints and prevents dehydration.

When you feel thirsty, this is a sign your body is already beginning to experience dehydration and is crying out for water. Prevent this from occurring by drinking water consistently throughout the day. Symptoms of dehydration can include headaches, lack of concentration, dry mouth, tiredness and lethargy. Insomnia can also be caused by dehydration, so if you're unable to sleep at night, try drinking more water the following day and see if this makes a difference.

Drinking two litres of water should be enough to keep the average person hydrated, though it would be great to get three litres into you while you're on this plan. Certain foods, in particular fruit and vegetables, can add to your daily water intake. Some fruits, e.g. watermelon, contain more than 90 per cent water, and consuming such foods on a regular basis can help boost your hydration levels. You should drink more water when you exercise, when it's very hot or when you have a fever, or if you're suffering from diarrhoea or vomiting.

Water and water alone is enough to provide adequate hydration. Other fluids may assist with hydration but can also provide elements which the body will need to process, eliminate or store, e.g. additives, preservatives, sodium and sugar. The only exception is herbal teas, which can count towards your water intake.

Tina's Top Tips for increasing your water intake:

1. Keep a water bottle in your car (away from the sun!), at your desk, in your handbag and on your bedside table at all times.

2. Replace all carbonated drinks in your diet with water (add lemon for flavour).

3. First thing in the morning have a glass of warm water with some freshly squeezed lemon juice (room-temperature water is OK if you're like me and don't like lemon in hot water).

4. Ensure you have water with you when exercising, at the gym or playing sports.

5. Eat your water! Increase your consumption of foods that contain water, such as cucumber, watermelon, grapefruit and celery.

6. Drink herbal teas.

7. Add freshly squeezed lemon juice, pink grapefruit, some frozen fruit, mint or cucumber to your water to make it tastier.

ACTIONS

1. Make sure you know the difference between good and bad carbs and what to eat and what to avoid.

2. Make sure you know the difference between good and bad fats.

3. Pay attention to how much processed food you eat and how much hidden sugar and wheat might be in your diet.

4. Pay attention to your water intake.

4

THE ENEMIES: WHEAT, SUGAR AND PROCESSED FOODS

In this chapter you'll learn:

- Why you should avoid wheat and gluten.
- Why sugar is so bad for you.
- Why you should stop eating processed foods.
- How to stop eating sugar and processed foods.
- How to read food labels – this is a key skill you *must* learn.

If you want to lose weight, the simplest way to do it is to cut out all wheat, sugar and processed foods. Trust me, that's all there is to it. These three bad guys tend to like to stick together, so you will find that if you cut out sugar, you will have to avoid most things with wheat (bread, pastries and crackers) and most, if not all, processed foods, because processed foods are full of sugar. Or if you focus on cutting out processed foods, you will automatically cut out all wheat and sugar. Processed foods, with all their additives, are the foods that make us sick and overweight.

I know I make it sound simple, but I'm aware that it's not. Many people these days rely so heavily on processed foods that leaving them out would be a huge change and they wouldn't know what to eat instead, so it's best to make these changes slowly for a lasting lifestyle change.

WHY IS WHEAT SO BAD?

Wheat is everywhere – bread, pasta, breakfast cereals; it's even in many ready-made sauces. Many people eat huge amounts of wheat at every meal without thinking twice about it – toast or cereal for breakfast, a sandwich for lunch, pasta for dinner.

Wheat is a major player when it comes to weight gain. It causes water retention, appetite stimulation and, like all simple (bad) carbohydrates, it makes your blood sugar levels rise, causing your body to produce insulin, which in turn promotes fat storage.

Many people find it difficult to digest wheat. This is due to the presence of gluten, which is a protein found in grains including wheat, rye, spelt and barley. The gluten in wheat is particularly strong, which is why many people are sensitive to wheat while being able to tolerate other grains, such as spelt and rye. Gluten is what makes bread so chewy and pizza dough so stretchy.

Some people suffer from an autoimmune condition called coeliac disease, which makes them allergic to gluten and unable to tolerate even the smallest quantities. Others, while not coeliac, have a sensitivity to gluten which can lead to similar symptoms, such as bloating, gas, dark circles under your eyes, persistent skin rashes, lack of energy and diarrhoea. Gluten has also been linked with health conditions such as eczema, depression, anxiety, migraines and neurological diseases.

It is important to point out that although a product may say it is gluten free, that does not automatically mean it is healthy. As with everything, read the label before you decide whether or not to purchase.

A big problem with wheat is that it's found in many unhealthy, processed foods such as cakes, bread, pastries, biscuits and crackers. These products are often high in sugar and have absolutely no nutritional value – in fact, it's just the opposite: they are very bad for you. Leaving out all these unhealthy wheat products will open your diet up to much more nutrient-rich and healthy foods, which will significantly improve your health and weight.

More and more people are cutting out wheat from their diet and there are many alternatives to wheat on the market now. Try almond, coconut or rice flour. You can even make biscuits from a tin of chickpeas! Quinoa is a fantastic wheat-free grain that can provide a tasty and nutritious alternative to pasta in your evening meal. Other carbohydrate food sources that provide healthy alternatives to wheat include sweet potato, millet, buckwheat, polenta, brown rice and oats.

SUGAR – YOUR BIGGEST ENEMY

Sugar is probably the biggest threat to our health in today's world. Some doctors are calling for laws to restrict sugar in the same way as the laws that control alcohol and tobacco.

One of the most obvious reasons why sugar is detrimental both to your general health and fat-loss plans is the high calorie content of most sugary foods. These foods contain vast amounts of calories yet offer little in terms of nourishment and satiety, making them easy to over-consume and binge on.

There are several books about sugar and the health problems it causes, including weight gain, and it is regularly in the news headlines. In the UK a group of doctors, medical professors and other experts have formed the pressure group Action on Sugar (actiononsugar.org) to put pressure on the government and the food industry to reduce the amount of sugar in processed foods. There is no escaping the fact that sugar is bad for you; in fact, it's probably much worse for you than you ever thought.

If you were to make one change and one change only to your diet, it should be to reduce your sugar intake; better yet, eliminate it. While the occasional sugary treat won't kill you, the fact is that most people do not keep sugary foods as an occasional treat but are consuming vast amounts of sugar each day at every meal, very often without even realising it.

The health effects of excessive sugar consumption

Excessive consumption of sugar has been identified as a risk factor in the development of type 2 diabetes because of its effect on insulin production. Blood sugar levels rise after consuming high-sugar foods; in response insulin is released to clear the glucose from your bloodstream into the cells of the body. As blood glucose levels drop, insulin secretion is reduced. However, if you are consuming high levels of sugar consistently throughout the day, you are constantly causing the release of insulin to regulate blood glucose levels. At some point the pancreas will stop responding and become insensitive to blood glucose levels, resulting in insulin-dependent diabetes.

Anti-aging experts have also linked sugar consumption with undesirable skin effects. A process called glycation is triggered by sugar consumption. Sugars in your bloodstream attach to protein and create a by-product called advanced glycation end products (AGES). These AGES can damage collagen and elastin, leading to wrinkles, sagging and less supple skin.

Excessive sugar consumption has also been shown to dampen the immune system and promote inflammation in the body, which can increase susceptibility to diseases and infection. Other negative health implications include Alzheimer's, cancer and obesity, as well as tooth decay, chronic fatigue, irritability, hyperactivity, insomnia, headaches, depression, high blood pressure, PMT and many more.

How much sugar is too much?

At the time of writing, the World Health Organization (WHO) has just called for the recommended maximum sugar intake level to be dropped to just 5 per cent of your daily energy intake; that is 25g, or six teaspoons. This includes all added sugars, meaning those natural sugars that are in honey, syrups, fruit juices and fruit concentrates. This is half the previous amount recommended. Six teaspoons of sugar might seem like plenty, but if you eat any processed foods, chances are you've exceeded this before lunchtime without even realising it. It is very difficult to find any processed foods that don't contain sugar. Ready meals such as pizzas, curries, pasta sauces, most condiments – they're all full of sugar. If you don't believe me, go to a supermarket and start reading labels – you will be shocked. And if you like soft drinks, you're in trouble, because one can of Coke contains 39g of sugar – that's ten teaspoons! My advice is to aim for as little added sugar as possible – zero would be ideal – with your entire sugar intake coming from fresh fruit and other naturally occurring sugars.

What is added sugar?

Surprisingly our intake of visible sugar, i.e. table sugar, has progressively decreased over the years, while consumption of 'invisible' added sugar is steadily on the increase. In essence, added sugar is anything that is added at any stage of the processing, manufacturing, cooking and eating process. The biggest offenders are heavily processed foods such as cakes, biscuits, confectionary, sauces, etc. Foods which have been refined have lost many of their original nutrients and add little to one's diet aside from sugar, fat and additives, leading to an expanding waistline.

Many people are unaware just how much of this added sugar there actually is in their favourite foods. When we talk about this in classes, people are usually shocked to find that, for example, a 30g bowl of the dieter's favourite, Special K, with semi-skimmed milk contains 11g of sugars and that sugar is the cereal's third largest ingredient – this is a supposedly healthy option, so you can only imagine what's in the less healthy options. Go to your fridge and kitchen cupboards right now and pull out a few items. Look at the listed ingredients and see if there's sugar in them.

Does sugar make you fat?

In short, yes. Sugar is the reason we are here today. We have touched on this already, but it's important, so let's go through it again.

All sugar, once consumed, is broken down rapidly and converted to glucose to be used as energy in the body. Any remaining glucose that is not used for immediate energy needs will be stored in the muscles and the liver. However, the body only has a limited glucose-storage capacity and any remaining glucose will be stored as fat. Furthermore, the presence of large volumes of glucose in the bloodstream following sugar ingestion stimulates the pancreas to release insulin. Insulin promotes fat storage in the body as it works to restore and balance the glucose levels of the bloodstream. This is why excessive sugar intake is a leading cause of obesity and weight problems.

What about fruit?

Many diet plans (Paleo in particular) today tell you to limit or even completely cut fruit out when trying to lose weight, but I cannot justify not consuming fruit. Yes it may contain sugar, but it is sugar in its natural form and part of a wholefood with fibre, vitamins, minerals, water and antioxidants. As a result the sugar in fruit is released more slowly into the bloodstream and it does not result in the same surge in blood sugar levels and subsequent rise and crash in energy. It is too valuable a food source for me to ever consider not having it as a staple part of my diet.

While some fruits can be high in sugar and it is often recommended that these are limited, I would not worry about this until you have cut all processed sugars out of your diet and been sugar free for at least four weeks. As long as you still struggle to resist cakes, ready meals and sweets, it is unnecessary to cut out fruit. Use fruit to replace unhealthy sweets instead.

Tina's Top Tips for fruit consumption:

1. Skip the juice and opt for the whole fruit.

2. Don't peel the skin – often a lot of the fibre will be contained in the skin.

3. Consuming fruit with a piece of protein or fat, such as a few nuts or nut butter, will further reduce the rate at which the sugar is released from fruit.

4. Having a piece of fruit can satisfy cravings for sugar and a sweet tooth.

5. Darker-coloured fruits tend to contain more antioxidants.

6. When it comes to the five-a-day fruit and veg recommendation, you should be eating more vegetables than fruit.

Is sugar addictive?

Some researchers claim that sugar is more addictive than heroin. You don't need to be a scientist to realise that it can certainly feel addictive – 'I just need my chocolate bar a day' is something I hear regularly. If you feel you really need something, that you can't live without it, that means you are, at least to some extent, addicted to it. If you think you're not, then prove it – go a month without. Whether the addiction is physical or emotional can be debated. I think it's often a bit of both, but probably more emotional. In fact, it has been found that intake of sugar is associated with the release of serotonin, a feel-good hormone.

Perhaps more easily identifiable is the sugar rush often experienced with high-sugar foods – the energy boost you get after eating a chocolate bar for instance. This is always short-lived, however, and a subsequent crash and burn is often felt. This leaves us tired, irritable, lethargic and maybe victim to headaches due to low blood glucose levels. So what do we do? We usually end up reaching for the biscuit tin again; it is a vicious cycle and one that is hard to break. So yes, in some ways sugar can be seen as addictive.

How to reduce your sugar consumption

It sounds simple: stop eating junk, stop eating processed foods, only buy natural wholefoods and cook everything yourself. In reality, however, this can seem impossible for many people.

The most important thing to do is to learn to read labels – this is very simple. All you have to check is whether sugar is listed as one of the ingredients and, if it is, how high on the list it is. Ingredients are always listed in order of quantity, so the higher up on the list sugar is, the more there is in the product. Keep in mind that sugar isn't always called sugar – it can also be called sucrose, mannitol, glucose, honey, lactose, fructose, sorbitol, corn syrup, malt, malt extract, maltose, molasses, golden syrup or invert sugar syrup. In most cases ingredients ending in the letters *ose* are sugar in disguise.

The first thing you should do is identify how much sugar you eat. Once you start your food diary you'll be able to do this easily. Often this is such an eye-opener that it shocks people into cutting out a lot of sugars. Going cold turkey can be hard, so take it one step at a time. Start by cutting down. Replace your regular comfort foods, like a bar of chocolate, with something lighter, like a flavoured yoghurt or a chocolate mousse, to help you break the habit; after a while move to healthy options like fruit.

It is often more about breaking the habit, the mental addiction, than anything else. A lot of people tell me that they just 'need' a biscuit with their mid-morning tea. In this case, I'd suggest replacing the tea with something else like herbal tea or water with lemon, thus helping you break the association between the tea and a biscuit. Or you might put the tea in a takeaway cup and go for a walk – you're not only cutting out the biscuit but getting some exercise as well! Another option is to prepare healthy alternatives to the biscuit. There are many that taste just as good but don't have the negative effects. For example, try some nut butter on an oatcake, maybe with a drop of maple syrup or sugar-free jam to sweeten it a bit. This is not only tasty, but also provides you with slow-releasing energy that keeps you feeling satisfied for longer than biscuits would. You also get some protein, which, as we learned above, is very important for weight loss and you should have it at every meal.

Look for sugar- and artificial sweetener-free alternatives. While most foods in supermarkets contain added sugars, more and more healthy alternatives come out all the time, so again, read the labels and do some research into your choices.

Learn to use sugar alternatives such as maple syrup, stevia (in its natural form) and xylitol in baking and food preparation. These sugar alternatives are all natural sweeteners and unlike refined sugar contain various vitamins and minerals which are beneficial to your health. That is not to say you can consume limitless amounts of them; they should only form a small and occasional part of your diet.

Tina's Top Tips for quitting sugar:

1. Glutamine is an amino acid which can help with sugar cravings. Take one tablespoon in a glass of water.

2. Chromium helps with sugar cravings by balancing your blood sugar levels. It can be found in foods such as eggs, nuts, asparagus and mushrooms, or taken as a supplement.

3. Eat some protein at every meal.

4. Cinnamon stabilises blood sugar levels; low blood sugar levels often cause cravings for sweet and sugary foods.

5. When you do eat sugar, eat it with some protein or fat. They will slow the release of sugar from the food, which will prevent surges in blood sugar levels.

PROCESSED FOODS AND YOUR HEALTH

Many foods undergo extreme levels of processing and commonly contain numerous sweeteners, colourings, flavourings, emulsifiers, thickeners and preservatives, resulting in a product which is far from wholesome and natural.

The more a food has been processed, the fewer nutrients it will contain. Many naturally occurring nutrients, such as vitamins and minerals, as well as fibre, are lost during processing and often other less healthy components, e.g. trans fats or sugars, will be added in. The reason for this processing is that it improves the taste and appearance of food and lengthens shelf life.

The processed food industry

Much time, effort and money is invested in advertising and marketing to present convenience and processed food as healthy. Labels may scream 'sugar free', 'fat free' or 'low calorie', but the ingredients list will tell a different tale. Trans fats, sugar replacements and an abundance of additives are more often than not present in vast amounts in such food products, all of which are bad for your health and well-being.

Convenience products are predictably high in calories, containing refined, nutrient-depleted ingredients. Ingredients used may often be low quality, synthetically formed and mass produced in low-income countries with little regulation. Vast amounts of money is spent to research ways and means of extending the shelf-life of products and on the manufacture of chemicals, additives and preservatives to improve flavour and reduce rancidity. Yet little thought or care is given to the health effects. The processed-food industry is based on profits and margins and is a big, powerful industry that has no interest in the health and welfare of the public. In the USA alone the industry is worth over $1 trillion, employs 16.5 million people and makes up 10 per cent of the country's GDP.

What is being added to your foods

- E-numbers and additives. These are ingredients added to food for various reasons, e.g. to make it last longer or to add flavour.

- Colours are used to make unappetising foods more attractive or to restore a natural colour to items which have lost their colour during processing.

- Preservatives prolong shelf-life and prevent bacteria growth.

- Emulsifiers, stabilisers and thickeners are used to enhance texture and prevent separation.

- Flavour enhancers.

- Glazing agents add shine and an attractive appearance to foods.

- Flour improvers and bleaches are used in baked goods and breads to improve texture and whiteness.

- Trans fats are added to many processed foods to improve texture, increase shelf-life and improve the flavour of products.

Low calorie, low fat, fat free – bad for your waistline!

Low calorie, low fat and fat free are all terms commonly equated with many convenience and ready meals. Such terms regularly snare dieters, who are drawn in by these low-energy foods, touted as being healthy and good for your waistline with the added bonus of no preparation needed. In reality, research has shown that those who regularly consume such foods actually end up eating more calories than non-convenience food eaters. The reason for this is the lack of satiety offered by these food products.

When we consume wholefoods which have remained largely unprocessed, a series of complex hormonal exchanges takes place. These send a signal to signify when we have consumed enough food for our hunger to be satisfied. The same does not happen when we eat processed junk. Processed foods contain large quantities of salt, sugar, trans fat and various other nastiness, disrupting the natural regulation of our hunger/fullness cycle. What results is a gross overconsumption of processed convenience foods before your body realises it has had enough. The digestion process is changed, along with the way nutrients are broken down by the body.

Consumption of highly processed, high-calorie foods can artificially stimulate dopamine (the pleasure neurotransmitter), which plays a role in addiction. The intake of such foods, which are lacking in nutrients and fibre, can result in the beginning of a food addiction due to the pleasurable feeling they induce. One is left craving more.

Protein, fat and fibre all promote satiety, fullness and satisfaction, but these components are more often than not lacking in convenience foods. Fat is very palatable and adds flavour and texture to foods; its removal means the food industry must compensate for the qualities which it contributes to food. In most cases fat is replaced with sugar or artificial sweeteners, which the body cannot utilise and which have no nutritional value.

How to choose what to buy

When it comes to eating for health, the main thing to remember when choosing food is to opt for nutrient-rich food at all times and to avoid empty calories as much as possible. Remember that the number one reason why we should eat is to fuel and nourish our bodies. So if you have a choice between an avocado, at about 160 calories, and a can of diet cola with its zero calories, which one do you think is better for someone wanting to lose weight? You're on a diet, remember. Look at each of them and ask, how is this going to nourish me? Avocados are full of fat – 100g of avocado has almost 13g of unsaturated and 2g of saturated fat; provides 28 per cent of your daily fibre needs; is rich in vitamin C, vitamin K, copper, folate, magnesium, vitamin B6, potassium, vitamin E; and contains some protein (2g) as well as calcium and iron. Avocado has a great many health benefits – it's good for cardiovascular health, lowers bad cholesterol, is an anti-inflammatory (so great for anyone suffering with arthritis, for example) and is excellent for your skin, among many other benefits. Above all, it's great for weight loss. The monounsaturated fatty acids in it are used as slow-burning energy rather than stored as body fat and you will feel full and satisfied for longer after your meal.

Diet cola is very appealing to dieters because it contains zero calories, but aside from that, what are the benefits of drinking this? You might think it tastes nice and is refreshing and that ad, 'I'm here for my 12 o'clock', made you giggle. It's fascinating how advertising works! It's also cheap and readily available, and quite often you might even win something. This is great marketing. Other than that, however, there are no benefits. Most diet colas are sweetened with aspartame, also known as E591, which is so bad for you it's banned in several countries. There are ninety documented symptoms caused by aspartame. These include headaches or migraines, dizziness, seizures, muscle spasms, rashes, depression, fatigue, irritability, insomnia, vision problems, heart palpitations, anxiety, loss of taste, vertigo, joint pain and weight gain (yes, the product promoted as good for dieters actually can cause weight gain!). Research has also shown that some chronic illnesses can be triggered or exacerbated by aspartame, for example, multiple sclerosis, epilepsy, chronic fatigue, Parkinson's, Alzheimer's, fibromyalgia and diabetes. Researchers in the University of Texas in San Antonio conducted a study of 1,500 adults and found, unsurprisingly, that there is a strong link between obesity and consumption of soft drinks. The interesting finding was that those drinking diet sodas had a higher chance of being obese than those who chose the regular option – for each can of diet soda consumed per day, the risk of obesity went up by 41 per cent!

So which one will you choose next time? The high-calorie avocado or the zero-calorie soda?

Soft drink substitute:

Try this refreshing drink next time you crave a soft drink. It has helped many of my clients quit their addiction:

Take half a pink grapefruit and squeeze the juice into a glass, top up with cold water, stir and enjoy.

A good rule to go by is to choose foods closer to the farm than the factory. The closer foods are to their natural state the less processed they are and the fewer artificial additives they contain. So avocado is perfect as it is 100 per cent natural. Diet soda, on the other hand, has absolutely nothing natural in it; it's made in a factory and is completely artificial.

At the core of any clean eating plan is the elimination of white starches, incorporation of wholegrains, avoidance of processed foods with additives and preservatives, and a focus on wholefoods such as fruit and vegetables. Remember to always read labels carefully, check the full ingredients list and don't trust any health claims that the packaging makes.

Tina's Top Tips for reducing your consumption of processed foods:

1. Read the ingredients list. If it is a long list of names that you have never heard of, never mind being able to pronounce, leave it on the shelf.

2. Avoid any product that contains high fructose corn syrup, sugar or trans fats.

3. Consume more wholefoods and by default you will find you are consuming less processed foods as you won't have room for them in your diet. Counting calories can become a thing of the past once the foods you are consuming are a product of nature as opposed to industry.

4. Cook for yourself: home-made versions of many processed ready meals are always far more tasty, nutritious and in most cases cheaper.

5. Experiment with healthy substitutes for processed ingredients, e.g. exchange white flour for coconut/almond/spelt flour and exchange sugar or artificial sweeteners for natural sweeteners such as honey or stevia.

6. When it comes to bread, pasta and rice, always opt for the wholegrain variety. However, make sure the product is in fact 100 per cent wholegrain. Check the list of ingredients to ensure that the product is not a combination of whole grains and refined white flour. Spelt is a great option.

What do I need to cut out of my diet?

Packaged cakes, biscuit, confectionary, etc.

Sugary breakfast cereals (there are very few sugar-free ones)

Ready meals (frozen and fresh)

Fizzy drinks

Processed meats

Canned foods high in sodium or containing sugar or additives

Jars of sauces and dressings

Fast food

Margarine

Artificial sweeteners

White bread, pasta, rice, etc. – any white flour products

WHAT ABOUT DAIRY?

Whether or not dairy is good for us is debated a lot. More and more research is emerging that dairy is not an essential part of the human diet and that it perhaps causes more harm than good. I avoid most dairy because I just don't think it's good for me and it's certainly not necessary – the exception to this is natural yoghurt. We humans are the only species that continue consuming milk after weaning and we take it from another species! An interesting fact to note is that osteoporosis rates are highest in the countries that have the highest dairy consumption (USA, England and Sweden), while countries such as Japan and China, where dairy consumption is low, have low osteoporosis rates. This is not to say that dairy is completely evil and you should avoid it – there is always more to the story – but drinking milk certainly doesn't seem to prevent osteoporosis as is commonly believed.

Ultimately, it comes down to balance – a balanced intake of all nutrients. No matter how much calcium you ingest, if your diet is bad it's not going to help much. Moreover, many dairy products are highly processed and contain added sugars, for example yoghurts and chocolate milks – these are not going to protect anyone's bones!

For those suffering from lactose intolerance, dairy is obviously out of the question. Some people suffering with respiratory conditions find that consumption of dairy foods can worsen their symptoms and they are advised to avoid dairy foods if this is the case. Sinus infection is a common condition that is often improved by leaving out all dairy (and wheat).

For others, consumption of moderate amounts of dairy foods will not be harmful to their health, but it is good to know that some dairy options are healthier than others and certainly better for weight loss.

What milk should you drink?

Whole milk is always better than semi-skimmed or skimmed – the fat content is likely to leave you feeling fuller and more satisfied and less likely to nibble on a biscuit. In reality if you drink only a glass or two a day the calories saved by choosing skimmed milk will be approximately twenty-five to forty, which, in the grand scheme of things, is not significant. It's even less significant if you only take a drop in your tea or coffee. Never choose skimmed milk, as the vitamins in dairy are fat soluble and when the fat is removed the body cannot absorb any of the remaining vitamins. Organic milk has also been shown to contain more nutrients than non-organic, so if you have to have milk opt for full (or low) fat and organic.

I would encourage you to try goat's milk. I have to admit, I'm not a fan of the strong taste, but my little girl loves it. It is non-mucus forming (hence it won't contribute towards sinus issues or other respiratory issues). It is less allergenic, easier to digest and a great source of nutrients; in fact it is slightly higher in protein than cow's milk. So if you suffer from respiratory issues, goat's milk and yoghurt are a great, nutritious alternative for you.

There are also other great milk alternatives to try, such as coconut milk, almond milk and hazelnut milk. Just remember to look at the label and make sure there's no added sugar. I have recently discovered almond lattes. Coffee is the only thing I want real milk in – alternatives just don't do it for me – but my local coffee shop has started serving lattes with almond milk, which are just delicious with a dash of cinnamon on top.

What about yoghurts?

Yoghurt aisles are one of the places where the real fooling of the innocent consumer happens. It pains me to see some of the slogans on yoghurt tubs – they all sound so good, but the fact is, most of them are rubbish (see 'Understanding Food Labels' p. 97). There are exactly two choices you have in the yoghurt aisle if you want to be healthy – plain natural yoghurt or Greek yoghurt (*not* Greek style). Flavoured yoghurts, in particular low-fat flavoured yoghurts, are nothing more than a sugar bomb packed with colourings, flavourings and preservatives. This is true even of the ones that say 'made with real fruit' – does it still look like real fruit? It might have been real at some point, but after all the processing it goes through, real it's not. And yoghurts for kids? These are some of the worst out there. Anything that's targeted at kids tends to be pure rubbish and yoghurts are some of the worst offenders.

It is so easy to add your own flavours to natural yoghurt at home by adding fresh fruit, berries, nuts, seeds etc. When it comes to low-fat or full-fat natural yoghurt, I always go for full-fat – it is lower in sugar, guaranteed to curb my hunger and in addition the vitamins are fat soluble, meaning that in order for the body to absorb and utilise them they must be consumed with fat. It all really comes down to the satisfying effect of the full-fat on our appetites. You're likely to eat a smaller portion of the full-fat variety than the low-fat version and keep your appetite under control for longer.

What is the difference between Greek yoghurt and Greek-style yoghurt?

All yoghurts are made by fermenting milk with live bacteria cultures. Traditional Greek yoghurt is created through a process that involves an extensive straining method that filters out excess water, which makes the yoghurt thicker and higher in protein than other typical yoghurts. The straining process removes the liquid whey, which results in the thick consistency. As it is more concentrated than conventional yoghurt, it packs in more protein per gram than other yoghurts. It is also lower in sugar and carbohydrate, as the lactose (milk sugar) is removed with the whey. Greek yoghurt can be more expensive than other yoghurt as it takes more milk to make it. The ratio of milk to yoghurt in the creation of Greek yoghurt is 4:1, while non-Greek yoghurts have a milk to yoghurt ratio of 1:1. Greek-style yoghurt is often made with standard yoghurt which has additives and thickeners to give it the same thick and creamy consistency as Greek yoghurt. It is always better to choose the real deal or, if you can only find Greek-style yoghurt, go for natural (full fat) instead.

Is butter healthy?

Butter is by far the superior choice when compared with margarine and various vegetable spread alternatives. It provides a valuable source of vitamins A, D, E and K2 along with omega 3 fatty acids, CLA (conjugated linoleic acid) and butyrate acid. Butter from grass-fed cows provides the most nutrients, in particular higher levels of omega 3, CLA, K2 and butyrate acid, when compared to grain-fed herds. CLA has been shown to help the body build muscle and reduce the amount of fat stored and has now become a popular supplement. Butyrate acid is a short-chain fatty acid which is also produced in the intestine by the gut flora. It has been linked with fighting inflammation in the body and improving digestive health.

In contrast margarine and other butter substitute spreads are made from cheap ingredients such as vegetable oils, emulsifiers, artificial colourings and flavourings and are highly processed and synthetically manufactured. Margarine in the past contained trans fats, the one type of fat which everyone should be avoiding. When the negative health impacts of trans fat became widely publicised, many margarines were reformulated without trans fat. This, however, does not improve the health benefits in any way and in fact manufacturers can label their margarine as trans fat free if it contains less than 0.5g per serving, so beware – even if it claims to be trans fat free, it may not be. If the word hydrogenated is in the list of ingredients this indicates that trans fats are present.

For years we were told to avoid butter due to its saturated fat content. But the link between saturated fat and heart disease is slowly becoming outdated and it is now believed we can enjoy small amounts of saturated fats in our diet without it having a detrimental impact on our health. My advice is to get rid of any margarine and vegetable spreads and choose real butter, in moderation of course. Another great alternative to try is coconut oil, which is what I mostly use instead of other spreads. The thing to remember, again, is that our bodies are designed to consume real wholefoods, not food which has been processed beyond recognition and to the point where it has lost all nutritional benefit and can actually be harmful to our health. Apply this concept to all foods you choose and your health will immediately improve and weight loss will follow.

What about cheese?

As with most foods there are better choices, and I take a similar stance on cheese as I do with other dairy foods. Although we now know that saturated fat is not as bad for our health as it was previously made out to be, it is still a fat we only want and need very small amounts of in our diet. For this reason the only cheeses I would eat are ricotta, buffalo mozzarella, goat's cheese, feta and cottage cheese, all of which are lower in fat and hence more easily digested than most hard cheeses such as cheddar. Of course it goes without saying that any processed cheese, or what I like to call fake cheese, such as Easy Singles, is off the menu!

WHAT ABOUT COFFEE AND BLACK TEA?

I for one could not go without my cup of coffee in the morning, and the good news is that you don't have to either. Once caffeine is not consumed in excessive amounts it can actually have some benefits. The problem often arises when too much is consumed and also depends on the form in which it is drunk. It is important to note that caffeine is a stimulant and when drunk in large quantities can lead to insomnia, stomach upset, an increased heart rate and restlessness, and may inhibit the absorption of nutrients.

On the other hand moderate amounts of caffeine have been associated with increased alertness and concentration. We all know how that afternoon coffee can perk us up for the last few hours of work. Consuming caffeine before exercising can boost your physical performance and increase your endurance. Recent studies have also associated caffeine consumption with a reduced risk of diabetes.

It's often what's added to your coffee, or what you have with it, that is the problem, so avoid adding sugar, flavoured syrups, whipped cream and of course the obligatory muffin or biscuit which so often go hand in hand with your mid-morning cuppa. All of the above offer no nutritional benefits and are merely a source of extra empty and unneeded calories. The best coffee option to go for in a coffee shop is plain old Americano or espresso. If, like me, you don't like black coffee and prefer it on the milky side, ask for an almond latte. Instead of sugar, sprinkle your coffee with cinnamon – this is great for balancing blood sugar levels and reducing cravings. Limit your coffee or black tea intake to one to two cups a day, and if you find caffeine can affect your sleep, avoid coffee in the afternoons.

UNDERSTANDING FOOD LABELS

If there is one skill I would love you to take away from this plan, it's how to read labels. If that's all you learn from this book, and if it's something you start doing regularly, I will be very happy! You need to be aware of the fact that the front of any food packaging often says one thing (usually, implying that the product is healthy) but very often, when you look at the small print on the back, the truth is very different.

Many people in my classes are horrified when they realise that their favourite 'health' products are far from healthy; it's all just clever marketing. Products aimed at kids are particularly cleverly marketed and are often far from what they claim to be.

On the back of any product you will see two different tables – the ingredients list and nutritional information. The ingredients of a food product are required to be listed on the label by law. Most people look at the nutritional information first, checking calories and maybe fat, when in fact the most important place to start is the ingredients list, which will tell you what's actually gone into this product.

The ingredients label

Explaining how to read food labels is best done by using an example and here's a typical cereal targeted at dieters. This is the ingredients list:

Ingredients

Rice, Wholewheat, Sugar, Barley, Malted Barley Flour, Barley Malt Flavouring, Salt, Vitamin C, Niacin, Iron, Vitamin B6, Vitamin B2 (Riboflavin), Vitamin B1 (Thiamin), Folic Acid, Vitamin D, Vitamin B12.

Allergy Information: Contains Wheat and Barley. May contain Milk.

Suitable for vegetarians, Halal.

Not Kosher.

And here is what that is telling you:

- The ingredients are always listed in order of descending weight, so the main ingredient is first. The main ingredients, therefore, are rice and wheat, followed by sugar. If you read the nutrition chapter carefully, you'll know that none of these are actually very nutritious ingredients.

- This is a good example of a heavily processed product, to the extent that it needs to be fortified with vitamins to improve the nutritional value. By choosing fresh, unprocessed and whole foods you are going to be providing your body with natural sources of vitamins and minerals without compromising your health or weight.

- Sugar is the third ingredient listed. This gives a good indication that this cereal is high in added sugar.

The nutrition label

By law (in Ireland) manufacturers are not required to display the nutritional information of a food product unless they make a health or nutritional claim regarding the food, for example that it's low fat. When provided, this information is given per 100g/100ml and in some cases also per serving. Nutritional labelling is any information provided on the label about the energy content and key nutrients in the food.

When comparing the nutritional content of different food products it is best to compare the values given per 100g rather than per serving size, as servings sizes can vary between manufacturers.

The nutritional information from a typical diet cereal is:

	Typical Value per 100g	per 30g serving with 125ml of semi-skimmed milk
ENERGY	1588kj/375kcal	727kj /172kcal
PROTEIN	9g	7g
CARBOHYDRATE	79g	30g
of which sugars	17g	11g
starch	62g	19g
FAT	1.5g	2.5g
of which saturates	0.3g	1.5g
FIBRE	4.5g	1.5g
SODIUM	0.4g	0.18g
SALT	1g	0.44g

And here is what that is telling you:

- **Energy (kj and kcal)** indicates how much energy (i.e. calories) is provided by the food. The number of servings you consume will determine the number of calories you take in. The average woman is said to need around 2,000 calories daily, although this figure varies from person to person depending on age, sex, height, weight and activity levels, so this should be considered only a very general guideline. It is good to check the calorie content, but this should not be the one you make your purchase decision on – think back to our example of diet cola versus an avocado.

- **Carbohydrate** indicates the total amount of carbohydrate in grams and also how much is sugars. Information is also provided on how much of the total carbohydrate is starch (this is not given in all cases). There is no differentiation here between naturally occurring and added sugars. To determine if a product contains added sugar you must look at the ingredients list. In the case of this cereal we know that it does contain added sugars. The lower the sugar content relative to the total amount of carbohydrate the better. An interesting fact to be aware of is that 4g of sugar is 1 tsp of sugar – keep this in mind when looking at how much sugar is contained in foods. Anything less than 5g per 100g is considered a low sugar content, while 15g or above per 100g would be a very high sugar content, so if you do decide to buy something with added sugar, keep these quantities in mind.

- **Fat** indicates the total amount of fat in grams contained in the product and the amount of it that is saturated fat. It is easy to then work out how much unsaturated fat is in the product by subtracting the saturated fat figure from the total fat figure. Up to 3g per 100g for total fat content is low, while 17g or more is high. A low saturated fat content would be 1.5g or less, and anything above 5g per 100g is high. This cereal is low in both total fat content and saturated fat. This might seem appealing to dieters, but in reality it is good to eat some fats at breakfast time, as this will fill you up better and keep your blood sugar levels stable for longer, as fats take longer to digest and so prevent cravings.

- **Fibre** indicates the total amount of fibre in the product. The average person should consume a minimum of 18g of fibre a day. High fibre foods are important for digestive health and healthy bowels. Foods containing 3g or more of fibre per

100g are generally considered to be a good source of fibre, while foods containing 6g or more per 100g are considered high fibre. Based on this, this cereal is a good source of fibre.

- **Sodium**. Although the above label lists both the sodium and the salt content, some labels only list the sodium content. But if you are aware of the following conversion – 1g of sodium is equal to 2.5g of salt – you can easily work out the salt content, i.e. you need to multiply the sodium content by 2.5 in order to get the actual salt content. Low sodium content would be 0.1g or less per 100g and high would be 0.6g or more per 100g. This cereal contains 1g per 100g, making it high in sodium. The average adult's daily intake of salt should be no more than 6g per day.

For me, reading labels and making a purchase decision is simple. The only question I ask is whether sugar is added, and if the answer is yes I won't buy it. That means 95 per cent, if not 99 per cent, of products I pick up in a supermarket, I put back. Mind you, once you've done your initial label reading, you'll soon learn to know the few products you can buy and you'll head straight to them, which makes shopping easier and faster, because you know the few aisles you need to go to. In recent years, more and more sugar-free products (that haven't been sweetened with artificial sweeteners) have started to pop up in supermarkets, which is great to see.

Other popular health food labels

Activia Fibre Cereals are marketed as a perfect way to kick-start your day and a great source of fibre – 'Everybody needs fibre every day'. A pot contains 15 per cent of your daily fibre needs.

These are the listed ingredients: yoghurt with Bifidus ActiRegularis® (whole milk, skimmed milk powder, cream, yoghurt cultures), sugar (6.5%), fibre (oligofructose, inulin), cereals 1.5% (wheat flake (0.7%), oat flake (0.5%), wheat bran (0.3%)), barley malt extract syrup (0.8%), concentrated grape juice, dried coconut, acidity regulators (lactic acid, calcium lactate), flavourings, stabilisers (pectin, xanthan gum), colour (caramel).

Note that sugar is the second highest ingredient. One hundred grams of yoghurt contains 13.7g of sugar. One serving is 120g, so that contains 16.4g sugar (over four teaspoons or one tablespoon). Remember that the recommended maximum intake should be 25g or six teaspoons. There's 3g of fibre per 100g which makes it an OK source of fibre, but there are better alternatives.

Healthier alternative: plain yoghurt with fresh fruit and some flaxseed or chia seeds for fibre.

Petits Filous is for children and is a prime example of focused marketing, concentrating only on the good. According to their website: *'Petits Filous provides your child with the goodness of calcium and Vitamin D, which, as part of a healthy diet and lifestyle, are critical for strong bones.'*

Yet sugar is the second highest ingredient and a 90g pot of this stuff contains 10.7g of sugar, which amounts to two and a half teaspoons. That is a lot for an adult but for a child it's even more – the American Heart Association recommends that children aged between four and eight consume no more than three teaspoons of added sugar daily.

It's worth noting that *all* flavoured yoghurts are very high in sugar and should be avoided.

Healthier alternative: Plain yoghurt with some stewed apple or pear (see my recipe, p. 314). Add a drop of maple syrup if you prefer it sweeter.

Probiotic yoghurt drinks are another product many people take because they think they're good for you. These are advertised as being full of vitamins, calcium and friendly bacteria and hence great for your immune system. However, depending on the brand and flavour, a small 100g bottle can contain between 10g and 13g of sugar. Sugar is not good for your immune system!

Healthier alternative: Start your day with a glass of water and lemon instead.

Flavoured waters. Many people buy these because they don't like plain water. A 500ml bottle of fruit-flavoured water can contain up to 24g of sugar. That is eight teaspoons. There are now sugar-free versions available, but these contain artificial sweeteners that are often worse than sugar for your health.

Healthier alternative: You can easily make your own flavoured water by adding lemon, grapefruit, cucumber, mint or frozen fruit to a bottle of water.

Fruit smoothies came under a lot of fire recently due to their high sugar content, and rightly so – a typical 250ml bottle contains an average of 26g of sugar. Many people buy these drinks thinking they are choosing the healthy option, and many also buy them for their kids, not realising that these are so high in sugar. Even a small 180ml kid's carton can contain 16.9g of sugar – over four teaspoons.

Although smoothies like this are made of 100 per cent fruit, they still have to go through a heavy manufacturing process which kills off many nutrients, and very little of the fruit's fibre is left in the end product.

Healthier alternative: Buy water when you're out and about and make smoothies at home. Get a good blender (though you can start with just a hand-held one), use berries (frozen are great!) or other fruit, some spinach, healthy oils, chia seeds, etc. and blend with some water or a milk alternative such as almond milk for a cheaper and healthier version.

Healthy crisps are one of my pet peeves. Firstly, there is no such thing. Secondly, a lot of these are actually not healthy at all. In a typical bag of vegetable crisps there's very little vegetable left – instead they've used ingredients like potato starch, potato flakes, corn flour, whey powder and added sugar and flavourings. The front might make you believe that it's a healthy, wholesome product but never, ever skip reading the back label to find out the truth.

Healthier alternative: If you really must have crisps go for the real thing – choose a good-quality product made of just potatoes, oil and sea salt. Ideally, of course you'd avoid all crisps. Homemade popcorn is a great savoury snack too – make it in a pot, not a microwave.

These are just a few examples of misleading marketing that demonstrate the importance of reading labels. In the future, don't buy anything without doing this. You'll find that just reading the labels and realising what is in them puts you off many products. Also, be aware that just because something is organic, that doesn't mean it's healthy – there can still be additives and a lot of sugar in these products. It might be organic sugar, but it's still sugar. Gluten free is another one to watch out for. Just because a product is gluten free doesn't mean it's healthy, and like organic produce, it can still be loaded with sugar or other additives.

Tina's Top Tips for reading labels:

1. Look closely at the amount of sugar and always check for added sugar. Remember, the lower the sugar content the better. Ideally, avoid any foods that have sugar listed as an ingredient, but if that's not possible then avoid any food which has sugar listed in the top three ingredients.

2. Check how many servings are in the package and what the standard serving size given by the manufacturer is. In most cases there are several servings in a pack, so bear this in mind when consuming the food and working out the nutritional information.

3. Check the fat content and, most importantly, check for the presence of trans fats.

4. Always go for foods which are closer to the lower end of the limits given for sugar, salt and fat as listed above.

5. Generally speaking, if a food contains a long list of ingredients, many of which you cannot pronounce, you are better off leaving it on the shelf.

ACTIONS

1. Look at your food diary and highlight any

    a. processed foods

    b. foods containing sugar

    c. wheat.

2. Start cutting down on these slowly, working to eliminate them from your diet over several weeks.

3. Observe the changes in how you feel as your diet improves. You will feel amazing!

4. Clear out your fridge and cupboards. Read labels and see what products need to be replaced with healthier alternatives.

5

HOW TO EAT

In this chapter you'll learn:

- Why it is important to eat enough and eat regularly.

- How to control your portions easily.

- What superfoods to add to your diet.

It is not just important to make sure you eat the right things (and leave out the wrong things); how you eat is equally important. Many people, when trying to lose weight, resort to skipping meals and dramatically restricting calories, thinking this is going to speed up weight loss. However, quite often this has the opposite effect and it's a very unhealthy approach. Understanding the importance of eating smaller meals but eating often and eating enough is very important. At the same time, you need to control your portions and make sure you don't overeat. I'm going to teach you a very simple and natural way of doing this – the hunger/fullness scale.

ARE YOU EATING ENOUGH?

It is not uncommon for us to see people who are struggling to lose weight and it turns out they are not eating enough. I've been there myself after I was diagnosed with a thyroid disorder (Hashimoto's thyroiditis) that made me balloon! I went up four dress sizes in as many months. I was desperate to lose the weight, so I went on a detox. Only it wasn't a healthy detox where you just cut out all the crap and eat a balanced diet of wholefoods; it was the latest faddy detox (apparently Gwyneth was a fan). While it was based on healthy foods, it was *far* too restrictive in terms of calorie intake. So I was on this plan for two weeks (in hindsight, I think three days would have been great as a kickstarter), consuming little more than celery sticks and lemon water, with the occasional yucky liver-flush drink. In the end, I gained 5lbs. You can only imagine how devastated I was; there were tears!

Looking back, I was so foolish. I was already suffering from a condition that had brought my metabolism to a near standstill and this was not the way to get it to function again! And if your metabolism isn't functioning properly, you sure aren't going to lose weight, but I wanted a quick fix. The good thing is that after that I went to see a good nutritionist and started studying health and nutrition myself so I wouldn't make the same mistakes again.

Our bodies require a certain number of calories (energy) every day. This is known as your basal metabolic rate (BMR) – essentially the number of calories your body burns to maintain basic functions such as digestion, breathing and temperature regulation if you're just lying in bed all day doing absolutely nothing. BMR for the average woman it is around 1,500 calories.

It is vital that you do not have a daily calorie intake which is lower than your BMR as, to put it simply, your body will not have enough energy to function normally. In response your metabolism will slow down and your basic bodily functions will start to slow down too. If you consider, for example, your hair, skin and nails – they are all 'living' components and need energy and nutrients to be sustained. If you do not provide your body with the basic number of calories it requires, you will see the consequences manifesting in weak and brittle hair and nails, as well as dry, flaky and lacklustre skin. Your digestive system may not function at its optimal level, which will have negative health implications, and an ill-functioning digestive system can prevent healthy weight loss from occurring and also prevent your body from efficiently absorbing nutrients.

Having an inadequate energy intake below the level of your BMR can also affect hormone production and thyroid function, which will lead to further metabolic damage and can further sabotage one's weight-loss progression.

Reducing your calorie intake too much can put you in danger of pushing your body into starvation mode. Our bodies are quite efficient when they think food is in short supply – we have been genetically designed this way for times of famine, food shortage, etc. What happens is that the body becomes energy efficient with negative and undesirable outcomes. It protects and preserves its existing fat stores and subsequently draws on lean muscle mass for its energy needs. This effectively leads to a reduced metabolism and what this means is a reduction and slowing of weight loss. In addition the energy that you do take in is more likely to be stored as fat, as your body is unsure of when it'll next be fed.

The more muscle one has the more energy you will burn while at rest. When attempting to transform your body and health the aim should be to reduce fat while maintaining lean muscle mass. The occasional day when your calorie intake is low will not then have a detrimental impact on your overall weight loss; only when this becomes a common occurrence will your body begin to conserve its existing energy and hold on to its fat stores.

In addition if your food intake is inadequate, you will find it hard to maintain a balanced diet and obtain all the nutrients your body requires for optimal health and performance. A balanced diet is one where the individual meets all their nutritional requirements to support normal growth and development and maintain body functions, while maintaining a healthy body weight.

By eating healthily and focusing on healthy portion sizes you can easily achieve 1lb of fat loss a week. The more active you are, the more likely you are to reach the 2lb fat-loss mark each week. Exercise is a vital component of weight loss and is essential for maintaining muscle mass, which will keep your metabolism up.

Note that in the first week or two of any healthy eating plan you may find the scales showing several pounds of weight loss. This is normal as your body dispels any water it has retained in addition to fat. After the initial couple of weeks you should find you are consistently losing 1–2lbs per week.

THE IMPORTANCE OF EATING REGULARLY

The hunger hormone, ghrelin, is what drives and controls our appetite. Ghrelin spikes after periods of fasting, so for this reason it is vital that you eat at regular intervals. One thing I always encourage my clients to do is aim for three main meals and two snacks a day. People often think skipping meals and eating less will help them lose weight faster, but this could not be further from the truth. So if you are a meal skipper this is one thing you have *got* to change ASAP.

We have already discussed why eating too little can be bad, but why is it so important that you eat at regular intervals throughout the day? Research shows that those who eat breakfast and regular meals are more successful at losing weight than those who don't. They are also less likely to overeat throughout the day. If you think of your body and metabolism like a fire that warms a room, you want to keep the fire going all day to keep the room warm by adding small bits of wood regularly throughout the day, rather than burning it all at once. So to keep your fire burning all day, you should aim to eat and refuel your body on average every 3 to 4 hours. You can do this by having breakfast, lunch and dinner with two snacks in between.

When you go a long time without eating, your blood sugar levels drop, which leaves you feeling tired, irritable, hungry and sluggish. When you feel like this you are more inclined to make less healthy food choices and to overeat. Think about it – when that 3 p.m. slump hit what did you feel like having? The chocolate bar or the apple?

The key is to prevent these slumps from occurring and eating every 3 to 4 hours ensures that both your body and brain have a steady supply of energy throughout the day, meaning that they can work optimally.

Not leaving big gaps between one meal and the next means that your blood sugar and energy levels are going to remain constant and your metabolism won't slow down to preserve energy. A slowed metabolism is the last thing you want when weight loss is your goal. Research also shows that skipping meals can lead to you overcompensating at your next meal. You need to establish a regular eating pattern to prevent your blood sugar levels from becoming unstable, leading to hunger pangs and cravings for unhealthy foods. Being consistent with your meals can actually cause your body to become more efficient at fat burning. Start your day the right way by having a good healthy breakfast and in doing so you set the tone for the rest of your food consumption throughout the day.

The key message here is don't wait till you are hungry to eat!

PORTION CONTROL – THE HUNGER/FULLNESS SCALE

Portion control is the key to weight loss. Many people simply eat far too much. There are a lot of guides to how much a portion of this or that should weigh, but I don't want you to get too hung up on these – nobody wants to be weighing every bite they eat! Just remember your balanced dinner plate (half vegetables, a quarter protein and a quarter good carbs) and make sure you use a regular dinner plate; avoid any over-sized ones. For further guidance, you might use your hand as a guide:

- A portion of proteins, such as meat or fish, should be the size of your palm.
- Starchy carbohydrate portions, such as rice or pasta, should be no bigger than your fist.
- Fresh or lightly cooked vegetables can and should be eaten freely. Make sure you include plenty of dark greens.

It is also possible to find a more intuitive way of deciding how much you should eat, by learning to tune in to your body and listen to what it is saying. A great tool is the hunger/fullness scale, developed by Dr Barbara Craighead, which will help you do just that. The scale helps you determine whether you need to eat and, when you do eat, when to stop.

How to use the hunger/fullness scale

When you feel hungry or are eating, take a moment to rate your feeling of hunger or fullness on the following scale:

1: Very hungry; starving; desperate. Your stomach is 'screaming'.

2: Moderately hungry; ready to eat. Your stomach is 'talking'.

3: Mildly hungry; starting to get hungry. Your stomach is 'whispering'.

4: Neutral. You feel no sensations of hunger or fullness.

5: Mildly full. You feel satisfied.

6: Very full. Your stomach is beginning to feel a bit distended.

7: Much too full. Your stomach feels stuffed.

It's recommended that you stay between 2.5 and 5.5 – moderately hungry to mildly full. Avoid going down to 1 by having regular snacks. Remember that it takes 20 minutes for your brain to know that your stomach is full, so eat slowly and stop when you're moderately full. It is also important to always remember to chew well. You will feel fuller and more satisfied sooner and your food will be better digested too.

To be able to use this scale properly, you should always eat away from any distractions like TV, work, reading, etc., and instead focus on your food only. You will find that food tastes much better and this can work as a little meditation too, so you'll feel relaxed and refreshed after your meal.

Watch out for non-hunger cues such as stress, emotions (anxiety, sadness, anger, depression), habitual eating patterns (eating while watching TV, having a biscuit with coffee), seeing or smelling trigger foods (walking past the chipper) and social occasions. In these situations, always use the hunger/fullness scale to determine whether you're really hungry or not.

Another great trick is to only take half the amount of food you think you're going to want to eat. Eat this first and then take a little break to observe if you are still hungry. If you are still hungry, go and take a quarter of what you would normally take and again eat this slowly, take a break and then decide if you still want more. Chances are that you'll find you are satisfied long before you normally would be. Use the leftovers for the next day's lunch!

SUPERFOODS

We can't talk about food and a healthy diet without talking about superfoods. These can be confusing for people. Marketers can be very good at persuading you to believe that unless you start eating the latest expensive superfood, you can't really stay healthy or lose weight, so many people feel under pressure to buy these things (then leave them, forgotten, at the back of the fridge). There are some superfoods that I love; others, while they might be good, I won't bother with.

While there is no scientific definition of what constitutes a superfood, these are commonly classified as a category of foods which are for the most part low in calories, nutrient dense and offer extensive health benefits. Every week it appears that there is a new exotic superfood being presented to us, from acai berries to coconut water and everything in between. The good news is that superfoods do not have to be exotic or eye-wateringly expensive, and I am going to share with you some of my favourites, which will greatly benefit your health.

Avocado

Feared by many with a fat phobia, this fruit is one which should become a staple part of your diet. Providing over twenty essential vitamins and minerals, the avocado has been associated with preventing cancer, diabetes, heart disease and obesity. Half an avocado packs in over 3g of insoluble fibre and provides more potassium than a banana. It is a rich source of folate, making it a great food for pregnant women or those trying to conceive. The monounsaturated fats present in avocado can help increase your good cholesterol and satisfy your appetite. Not only is this fruit extremely good for you, but it is also super versatile. It's great in salads and smoothies, can be used as a substitute for mayonnaise, or as a basis for dips. You can even make a healthy chocolate mousse using avocado (trust me, it's delicious!).

Quinoa

A complete source of protein providing you with all the essential amino acids your body requires, quinoa was the staple diet of the ancient Incas. Not actually a grain but a seed, this superfood is gluten free and provides 5g of fibre per cup, ensuring that it will help keep your digestive system in full working order. The protein content, coupled with the fibre, is guaranteed to keep your hunger at bay. Not only this, but quinoa also provides a range of other nutrients, including iron, calcium, magnesium and vitamin B. Quinoa can become the main ingredient in all of your meals – serve it up in the form of porridge for breakfast, try a delicious salad at lunchtime and use it as a healthy alternative to rice or pasta come dinner time. Always rinse your quinoa before cooking to remove its outer coating (called saponin), which gives it a bitter taste.

Coconut oil

Having been given a bad reputation in the 1990s due to its saturated fat content, coconut oil is today celebrated in the nutrition world. It is now understood that the medium-chain fatty-acid composition of coconut oil means that it can be easily used by the body for energy rather than being stored as fat, as the body metabolises it in a different way from other fatty acids. Lauric acid is the main fatty acid which is present in coconut oil (40 per cent); this is renowned for its anti-bacterial, anti-microbial and anti-viral properties. When lauric acid is present in the body it is converted into a compound called monolaurin, which helps protect against bacterial infections. The only other natural source of such high concentrations of lauric acid is breast milk. Coconut oil has also been associated with improving cholesterol levels, aiding weight loss and strengthening the immune system.

Its use is not limited to the kitchen, however. This oil also makes a great hair conditioner and skin moisturiser, shaving aid, lip balm, massage oil and make-up remover, to name but a few of its other uses. Just ensure that the coconut oil you purchase is organic, cold-pressed and virgin.

Beetroot

Roasted, juiced or freshly grated, beetroot is a versatile root vegetable with powerful health benefits extending to protection against heart disease, birth defects and cancer. Pickled beetroot can be nice as well, but look for one that contains no sugar or other artificial additives. Beetroot has long been touted as a food with superpowers; the ancient Romans used to drink beetroot juice as an aphrodisiac, while the ancient Greeks offered beetroot up to their gods as a sacrifice. Beetroot contains an abundance of vitamins and minerals such as magnesium, potassium, folate, phosphorous, selenium, manganese, iron and vitamins A, B and C, all of which promote and contribute towards general good health and well-being. Drinking beetroot juice has been associated with lowering blood pressure. This is believed to be due to the presence of nitrates in the juice. Nitrates are converted to nitric oxide in the body, which relaxes and widens the blood vessels, effectively lowering blood pressure and allowing oxygen-rich blood to pump more easily around the body. In addition beetroot has also been acclaimed for its liver-detoxifying properties thanks to the presence of betacyanins.

A fun fact about beetroot is that consuming it can sometimes cause urine to turn pink or red in colour. This condition is called beeturia and is not considered harmful.

Eggs

You might never have considered eggs to be in the superfood category but do not underestimate the power of the humble egg. Guaranteed to be found in almost every kitchen, eggs are the one food I really could not live without. Eggs are relatively low in calories yet high in protein and a source of many nutrients. One average-sized egg contains approximately seventy-eight calories, 5g of fat and 6g of complete protein, i.e. all the essential amino acids. The protein content of eggs promotes satiety, meaning they will keep you feeling full – perfect for someone trying to reduce their body fat.

In addition to all of this, eggs also contain two antioxidants called lutein and zeaxanthin, which can help prevent age-related macular degeneration, a leading cause of blindness. Eggs are also a good source of vitamin B, vitamin D, vitamin A, selenium, iron and choline, which is a vital nutrient for the brain. Do not be tempted to discard the yolk, as it is the yolk which contains most of the nutrients! In the past, due to an association with cholesterol, we were advised to limit the number of eggs we consumed. However, this has since been dismissed, so we can happily consume eggs on a daily basis.

Chia seeds

Chia seeds were consumed by the Aztecs, Incas and Mayans for endurance and strength. Today I consume them on an almost daily basis, incorporating them into my diet in many different ways. When soaked in water chia seeds can swell up to fifteen times their original size, meaning that they can really keep you feeling full for hours after consuming them and so can assist weight loss in this manner. They are a fantastic source of omega 3 fatty acids, mainly ALA, which the body cannot produce itself and must be obtained from your diet. Omega 3 fatty acids can help reduce inflammation in the body. In addition chia seeds are a good source of protein, calcium, potassium, vitamin B and fibre, which will help control blood sugar levels and keep constipation at bay. Enjoy them in smoothies and soups, add them to porridge, sprinkle on salads or in my favourite form as chia pudding – made by simply soaking them in milk. For a little seed they pack a powerful punch of nutrition.

Garlic

I am a huge garlic fan and am always adding it to dishes. It becomes even more of a staple in my diet during the winter months, as garlic has been shown to reduce infections due to the presence of a compound called allicin. Allicin is released as the garlic is crushed. Garlic is also known for reducing cholesterol and blood pressure, improving circulation, and fighting inflammation and cancer. In addition to these health benefits, garlic also provides potassium, zinc, phosphorous, vitamin C and vitamin B. Nature's antibiotic, with anti-bacterial, anti-viral and anti-yeast properties, this is one superfood which you need to start utilising. One of my favourite ways to use garlic is to sauté it with some kale, combining two of my favourite foods! For optimum health benefits garlic is best consumed raw.

Salmon

Oily fish such as salmon are a great source of omega 3 fatty acids. Associated with reduced risk of heart disease, arthritis, Alzheimer's and inflammation, among a long list of ailments, omega 3 should be a vital component of everyone's diet. Fish is often referred to as brain food. This is certainly the case with salmon, as omega 3 has been linked with improving memory and increasing brain efficiency. Salmon is also high in protein, with 100g of salmon packing in 25g of protein. Salmon also provides vitamin D, which is needed for healthy bones and is also good for the immune system, and vitamins A and B. In terms of minerals, salmon provides us with iron, calcium and selenium. Other great oily fish with similar benefits to salmon include trout, mackerel, sardines and tuna. I try to eat oily fish at least once a week, but preferably twice, and you should do the same. Wild salmon contains more omega 3 fatty acids than farmed salmon, so choose wild when possible.

Berries

I consider berries to be nature's sweets. My favourite superfood berries are blueberries and raspberries. Both are rich in anti-oxidants, polyphenols and flavonoids. Blueberries and raspberries also contain fibre, as well as some vital vitamins – C and E, both of which are powerful antioxidants which work to prevent free-radical damage. Antioxidants can help prevent heart disease, cancer and premature aging among other things. They are low in calories and high in nutrients; what more can you ask for? Berries make a great sweet snack for kids as well. Fresh berries can be expensive at times, so a good tip is to buy frozen berries which are generally cheaper and just as nutritious.

Almonds

This humble nut has astounding nutritional properties. Full of healthy monounsaturated fats, almonds can help lower cholesterol and reduce your risk of heart disease. The protein content will be sure to curb your hunger, and a handful makes the perfect snack to bridge the gap between meals and hence can assist with weight loss. Almonds are also a good source of vitamin E, a potent antioxidant which promotes healthy skin and heart health. They also contain magnesium and potassium, two minerals which can help promote a restful night's sleep and aid muscle relaxation. They are quite an energy-dense food, however, so do practise portion control! Enjoy almonds in their whole form as a nut or try almond milk as a healthy dairy-free alternative – I love adding almond milk to my smoothies. Another favourite way of mine to enjoy almonds is as almond butter, which is delicious spread on an oatcake and topped with a few slices of banana.

Oats

There is no better way to start your day than with a bowl of oats. Oats are high in soluble fibre in the form of beta-glucan, which is very effective for reducing cholesterol levels in the body. In addition they also contain insoluble fibre which helps promote healthy bowels and prevent constipation, as it moves through the digestive system without being absorbed. The high fibre content of oats can add to a feeling of fullness after consumption and leads to balanced blood sugar levels, which can help prevent hunger and cravings, so they make an ideal breakfast for anyone on a weight-loss plan. Alongside their impressive fibre content, oats are also a good source of B vitamins, folic acid and magnesium, among other nutrients. B vitamins are essential for the release of energy from food. Enjoy oats hot in the traditional way during the winter months or in my preferred form as overnight oats (see recipe on p. 245) as an alternative in the warmer temperatures of summer. Avoid any packaged, flavoured quick oats, as these more often than not have sugar added in.

Tomatoes

Many of the superfood properties of tomatoes are owed to their lycopene content. Lycopene is a potent antioxidant which gives tomatoes their deep colour. Cooking tomatoes actually makes the lycopene more readily available to the body. Lycopene is fat soluble, so to ensure the body can efficiently absorb it, cook your tomatoes with a little bit of oil. It has been associated with prevention of cancers such as those of the stomach, lungs and skin. Lycopene has also been linked with lowering cholesterol, protecting against heart disease and improving vision. Lycopene is found in other fruits and vegetables but is most concentrated in tomatoes. Tomatoes are also a good source of vitamins A, C and E and also potassium. An antioxidant called lutein which promotes healthy vision by protecting the retina against damage by free radicals is also found in tomatoes. They are a super-versatile food and make a great addition to many meals; I add them to everything and often have them for breakfast, lunch and dinner. Generally the darker the colour of the tomato the more lycopene it will contain.

Flaxseed

Flaxseed may be small in size but it packs in a lot of nutrition.

Rich in omega 3 fatty acids, fibre and phytochemicals, flaxseed is something you should consume on a daily basis. It is the richest plant source of omega 3, and a 30g serving of flaxseed will provide you with 7.2g of omega 3 fatty acids. Omega 3 fatty acids are anti-inflammatory and have been associated with numerous health benefits, from heart health to neurological development to improving arthritis. Flaxseed contains both soluble and insoluble fibre, helping to promote regularity and lower cholesterol. Lignan, a phytochemical found in flaxseed, mimics the action of oestrogen in the body and may be beneficial to women going through the menopause, helping to reduce some of the associated symptoms. It is best to consume flaxseed which has been ground up, as it is more easily absorbed by the body in comparison with its whole form. Add flaxseed to porridge, salads, yoghurt, smoothies, soups, sauces and home baking – its uses are endless.

Cinnamon

One of the world's oldest spices, cinnamon has been associated with regulating blood sugar levels, which can help to control cravings and assist in weight loss and may be beneficial to those with diabetes. Further research is needed to establish just how effective it may be in the control of diabetes. One tablespoon of cinnamon contains just nineteen calories and an impressive 4g of fibre. It is a great source of manganese, with one tablespoon providing almost 70 per cent of the recommended daily intake. Manganese is an important nutrient for bone development, absorption of nutrients and wound healing, and it acts as a co-enzyme to assist metabolic activity in the body. Try it sprinkled in your coffee as a healthy alternative to sugar, or use it in your meals to add a little spice. I love it mixed in with my porridge.

Yoghurt

Yoghurt is one of my favourite superfoods; I eat it almost every day. Bear in mind I am not talking about flavoured yoghurts which are laden with sugar and additives, but pure natural or real Greek yoghurt. Thick and creamy, natural yoghurt is thought to promote digestive health due to the presence of good bacteria known as probiotics. Much of our immune system is centred in our guts so it is vital that we have the right balance of good and bad bacteria. Consuming probiotics regularly can assist in this. Natural yoghurt can also help you recover from a yeast infection. In addition to the above, a serving of natural yoghurt will provide you with calcium, protein, a little fat and B vitamins. Vitamin B12, found in natural yoghurt, is important for the formation of red blood cells and can help prevent anaemia. The protein and fat content of yoghurt makes it an essential food if weight loss is your goal, as it will satisfy your appetite and keep you feeling fuller for longer. Greek yoghurt is even higher in protein than natural yoghurt and is very low in sugar. Both natural and Greek yoghurt are very versatile and can be used as sauces, salad dressings or as a healthy alternative to mayonnaise. If you find plain yoghurt boring on its own, add your own flavourings such as chopped fruit, berries, nuts, seeds or a drizzle of honey to jazz it up.

Prunes

Prunes are somewhat of an under-appreciated superfood. Prunes are dried plums that contain large quantities of insoluble fibre and so they are an invaluable addition to the diet for anyone who suffers with constipation and will help promote a healthy digestive system. The soluble fibre found in prunes slows food transit time, promoting a feeling of fullness and aiding satiety. Prunes also have a high vitamin A and beta carotene content, both of which are vital nutrients to maintain healthy vision. They contain high levels of phytonutrients known as phenols. Phenols have been linked with protection against free radical damage; free radicals can cause damage to cells in the body, which can promote disease. The phenols in prunes which demonstrate these effects are called neochlorogenic acid and chlorogenic acid. Prunes have been found to contain high levels of antioxidants, even more than other superfoods such as blueberries. The vitamin C found in prunes can aid in the body's absorption of iron. In America prunes have actually been renamed dried plums to make them sound more appealing to people!

Spirulina

Spirulina is a blue-green algae which you can purchase in powder form. It was regularly consumed by the Aztecs centuries ago. Spirulina is abundant in vitamins, minerals and amino acids. It consists of over 60 per cent complete protein, meaning it contains all of the essential amino acids which are needed by the body, in addition to ten non-essential amino acids. Spirulina contains chlorophyll, which is known for its blood-cleansing properties. In addition, spirulina is a source of essential fatty acids such as gamma linolenic acid (GLA). GLA helps to modulate inflammation in the body. It also provides calcium, magnesium, manganese, zinc and vitamins C, A, E and B among other nutrients, and has been associated with boosting the immune system, improving digestion and increasing energy levels. It is easily digested and absorbed by the body. Try adding it to smoothies to give them the ultimate health boost.

ACTIONS

1. Look at your food diary and identify if you are eating regularly and enough.

2. Start using the hunger/fullness scale to control your portions.

3. Start adding a few superfoods to your diet.

6

THE PLAN

In this chapter you'll learn:

- What to do right now.

- How to make the most of your food diary.

- Lifestyle changes to make.

- What you should and shouldn't be eating.

I hope that by now you are raring to go and, more importantly, that you feel confident that you can do this – because you can! However, there may still be a voice in your head expressing doubt about whether you can do this or not – that's fine; just tell that voice you're going to prove it wrong. Take it one day at a time and for every good day, be proud! Your confidence will grow as you have one successful day after another. If you're still feeling completely negative and have more doubt than confidence in yourself, it might be a good idea to work on that first. Work on improving your lifestyle and your attitude before starting this programme. Remember also that if your life is currently extremely stressful and you already feel like you don't get a minute's break, you might want to consider whether now is a good time to start this. Is this going to add to your stress or relieve it? Eating well is good when you're stressed, but on the other hand, having to plan and prepare your meals when you don't have the time might make you more stressed and you might want to focus on learning to manage your stress first.

If you're ready to start, all the details you need will be in this and the next chapter. It might seem like a lot of information but it's really simple – you want to eat clean. Avoid processed foods, sugar and wheat. Eat lots of green veg, fruit, lean protein, good fats and some good carbs. Very soon this will become habit. You will spend quite a bit of time planning, reading labels and learning more about the food you eat in the beginning, but after a while, this will become the norm and it'll be very simple. Trust me, I went through this transition period myself, and when I think back I remember it being hard to figure out what to eat, whereas now, years later, what I eat is just, you know, normal stuff.

As you embark on this plan it's also good to remember that moderation is the key, as is making small changes one at a time. Do not try to be perfect from day one!

WHAT TO DO RIGHT NOW

1. Keep a food diary

If you are not already doing so, you should start keeping a food diary right now – whether you're eating really well or nothing but rubbish. This is your most important tool.

A food diary will help you understand your eating patterns, notice emotional eating and identify where you need to make changes. When you're not getting the results you think you should be, you can look at your food diary and analyse it according to the plan's guidelines. It should be pretty easy to see where you might be going wrong.

I really can't stress the importance of keeping a food diary enough. Statistics show that those who keep one achieve better results. Most often, when one of my clients' weight loss stalls, or when they put on weight, and I ask to see their food diary, the reply is, 'Well, I haven't been really good at keeping it ...' Once they get back on track with their diary, their weight loss gets back on track too.

You can also keep a food diary online by taking photos. Set up a blog or a Tumblr page and post a photo of everything you eat. You can set this up as a private page so that no one else can see it. Taking a photo of what you're going to eat is often enough to stop yourself from eating something bad.

How to keep a food diary

A food diary is simply a record of all food and drink consumed on a daily basis. There are several key things you should include in it:

- What you ate and drank.

- When/what time you consumed it.

- Where you consumed it – home, work, at your desk, in front of the TV.

- Why you ate – keep a record of your feelings/mood at the time.

How to make the most out of your food diary

At the end of each day or each week you need to sit down and take a good hard look at your diary to establish what you are doing right, where you are going wrong and why you eat the way you do. Once you have done this and established what your stumbling blocks are, you can come up with ways to combat them and you will then be well on your way to achieving your health and weight-loss goals.

Taking note of where you eat and how you are feeling every time you eat will make it easier to establish links. Here's how to analyse your food diary:

- **Time and frequency of eating:** look for patterns in the time of day and what you eat. Is there a certain time that you reach for the biscuit tin? Is there a particular point in the day when your eating habits go downhill? This is also applicable to particular days of the week, e.g. the weekend. Lots of people find that during the daytime they make healthy food choices but when it comes to the evening good intentions start to slip and they end up bingeing on sugary and fatty foods. Also take a look at how often you eat and how much time you leave between each meal. Are you skipping meals and ending up overcompensating later that day, or perhaps eating too much, too often of the wrong foods throughout the day, only to be left with no appetite for a nutritious dinner?

- **Specific foods that act as triggers:** can you identify any foods you consume which cause all your resolve to go out the window so that your eating spirals out of control? For example, did that one biscuit lead to two, then to half the pack? Did that one square of chocolate lead to half a family-size bar? Sugary, fatty and processed foods are the ones most likely to result in a binge or overindulgence.

- **Emotions:** can you link your mood and emotions at various points during the day to the food choices you made? Did something happen to make you reach for the chocolate – time of the month, stressful day, negative thoughts? This is one of the most important things to identify in order to change your eating habits. By establishing why you may overeat certain types of food, i.e. comfort food, you are making a massive breakthrough in gaining control over your life and weight.

- **Alcohol:** does alcohol reduce your resolve and give you unhealthy cravings, ultimately destroying your healthy eating plans and weight-loss progress? Try to establish any links between alcohol consumption and unhealthy food choices. Alcohol delivers a double whammy in that it lowers blood sugar levels, leading to hunger and sometimes unhealthy cravings, while also weakening our resolve and reducing our compliance with healthy-eating plans. Alcohol intake is something which needs to be seriously addressed when on any kind of healthy-eating/weight-loss journey.

- **Excuses:** do you find yourself making excuses for certain food choices? For example, it's the weekend so this bottle of wine doesn't count, or, I've had a bad day, so I deserve to eat this family-size bar of chocolate. Such habits may have become second nature, so much so that you do not even think twice about them and they are standard practice. Use your food diary to establish if you have any excuses for unhealthy habits that may be having a negative impact on your health and weight.

Specific food points to look out for

- **Are you drinking enough water?** You should be aiming for approximately 2 litres throughout the day, possibly more if you are exercising intensively or if the weather is particularly hot.

- **Are you consuming enough fruit and vegetables daily?** Aim for at least five portions daily, with the majority of these coming from vegetables. A good guideline is to ensure half your dinner plate consists of vegetables. Aim for servings at each meal, e.g. fruit with breakfast, salad with lunch and vegetables with dinner.

- **Have you eaten any fish this week?** We all should try and eat fish at least twice a week and ensure one of these is a serving of oily fish.

- **Are you consuming healthy sources of fat daily?** Do not be afraid of healthy fats such as coconut oil, olive oil, nuts, seeds, nut butters, oily fish, eggs, etc. Your body *needs* them and they are vital for both weight loss and optimum health.

- **How many sugary drinks are you consuming?** On this plan, one is too many!

- **Are you consuming too much of any particular food group?** For example, do the majority of your meals largely consist of carbohydrates or unhealthy fats from processed sources? Just as importantly, are you not consuming enough of any particular food group, such as protein or healthy fats?

- **Are you over-relying on a particular food?** For example, bread – toast for breakfast, sandwich for lunch and a night-time snack of more toast?

- **Are you missing out any key meals?** Do you skip breakfast? Is your eating centred around one part of the day? Do you go all day without eating and then fill yourself that evening by eating everything around you?

- **Are you having regular snacks during the day?** If so what kind of snacks are they? Are you pre-planning and preparing your snacks or do you find yourself getting caught out and resorting to a chocolate bar from the shop? This may be something you need to work on. You should have two healthy snacks a day to keep your blood sugar levels stable and your energy maintained between meals.

- **Is sugar your vice?** Closely look at your sugar intake, in particular your added-sugar intake. When embarking on a weight-loss plan a lot of people wrongly focus on reducing their fat intake. While it is important to reduce your fat intake from unhealthy sources, one of the most important things you need to focus on reducing is sugar. Consider your intake from every source, and yes those sugars in your coffee or tea do count.

- **Are there a lot of branded, labelled foods in your food diary?** Bear in mind natural, unprocessed and wholefoods in most cases do not require branding or labels, e.g. chicken, eggs, apples, broccoli, etc.

Once you have examined your current food intake and eating patterns you will be in a position to make the necessary changes to improve your health and promote weight loss.

2. Make gradual, small changes

Do not go cold turkey and try to be perfect from day one. Take one step at a time. Each week aim to make two or three changes to your diet. Small changes made over time will be more effective than trying to change everything at once. Remember, Rome wasn't built in a day! What changes you have to make, and how long it takes you to make them, depends on where you are starting from, how good or bad your diet is at the moment. Some examples of changes you might make:

- I will make time for breakfast every day this week.

- I will drink 2 litres of water each day.

- I will not leave such large gaps between meals and will factor in snacks instead.

- I will eat more vegetables.

- I will cut out all takeaways.

- I will cut out all ready meals.

- I will remove my daily can of Coke from my diet (things like this can be gradually removed to prevent withdrawal!).

- I will reduce my intake of wheat and gradually cut it out.

- I will reduce my intake of added sugar and gradually cut it out.

3. Make a plan

Planning is the key. It is absolutely vital that you make time for planning your meals for a week and doing a proper shop.

This is how I do it. On a Friday night or Saturday morning I sit down with my cookbooks and all my favourite recipes and write down breakfast, lunch and dinner for each day of the following week, Monday to Sunday – it is very important to plan for the weekends as well. I try to find at least one new recipe to try each week to keep things interesting, though some weeks I don't have time or don't feel like it. Then I just write down the usual, sometimes copying the previous week's plan, or I might try a variation of a favourite recipe. I try to find recipes that I can cook for dinner and then have some leftovers for lunch the next day at least a couple of times a week for when I'm busy. Breakfast is pretty much the same every day, though every now and then I get bored and fancy a change. For example, at the moment I'm having gluten-free granola with yoghurt and berries every morning and I love it. But up until recently I had porridge; before that it was green smoothies. You might want more variety and plan a different breakfast for each day.

I also write down snacks, even though most often they're simple things like nuts, dried fruit, crackers and hummus, but I write them down anyway.

While I'm writing this menu, I also have a second list going – a list of ingredients. I write down everything I need to buy. If I'm not sure if I have an ingredient (and unless I'm sitting in the kitchen and can easily get up and check), I write it down with a question mark next to it so I can check later.

I always write my lists on my phone. I use an app called Wunderlist where I have a list for shopping – that way I never forget my list because I have my phone with me all the time. You might also divide your list into different shops, e.g. greengrocers, health food store, supermarket. I'm lucky that I have all these shops right next to each other, so they're all easy to go to, but I used to have three lists (I love lists!).

Once I'm done, I stick the menu on my fridge door and do my shopping (you could do this online if you're short on time). Then, every day, I check what's on the menu for the next day and see if I need to prepare something in advance. Mostly there's no prep needed because I go for easy, quick recipes, but things like snacks can be put in containers, or something like a smoothie can be prepared the night before.

Being organised is really the key. I also have some extra emergency snacks (nuts and dried fruit) in my car, handbag and in my office, so when I'm stuck, I always have something healthy near me. It's those times you're stuck and not prepared that most of the damage is done.

4. Know your pitfalls
Recognise when and why you eat badly and tackle those situations. Your food diary will help you with this and keeping it for a week

before you start your plan will really open your eyes. You might also look at your dieting history – what went wrong in the past? Is there a pattern you can recognise? For example, did you find diets too strict? Then you know this time not to be too strict on yourself, to allow some flexibility and plan treats regularly, but be careful not to overdo it – you want to get results too!

You might know some of your pitfalls already. Evenings tend to be a risky time for many; others can't stop eating while cooking; and weekends can be a big challenge.

LIFESTYLE

These are the changes you might need to make, one at a time. Again, don't expect to completely change your lifestyle overnight; it's not possible and sometimes the circumstances don't allow big changes. However, becoming aware of these things will help you get started when you do have the time.

1. Sleep

Remember that sleep, according to some experts, is as important as your diet. Your body, including your metabolism, is not going to function as well as it can when you're tired, so you won't be losing weight as easily either. See chapter 7 for great tips.

2. Exercise and be active

Exercise is an important part of a healthy lifestyle. It is not only going to help you lose weight but also keep you strong and healthy. See chapter 8 for more details. Remember that it is not just exercise you need; increasing your general activity level is as important, so try to move as much as you can throughout the day.

3. Reduce stress

Whether you want to lose weight or not, excessive stress is not good for anyone. It will make you sick and it can make you gain weight. Read chapter 7 for more information and tips on how to reduce stress. Start with just one or two small things.

4. Stay focused and positive

Remember why you started; what is it that you want to achieve? Why do you want to make this change? Do your happy-weight visualisation every day or as often as you need – have that image firmly in your head. Nothing tastes better than feeling that good about yourself all the time! Have a read through chapters 1 and 9.

THE GUIDELINES – EATING
WHAT TO EAT

It's simple. You should eat a balanced diet in which you're eating all the food groups and all vitamins and nutrients in the right quantities – thus it's balanced. Any bad stuff disturbs that balance. A balanced diet consists of wholefoods only, food as natural and close to its original form as possible. I often think of it as food with minimum labels – I would say packaging but everything is packaged these days, even fresh food. If most of the things you buy have an ingredients label, your diet is not very balanced. I think maybe about 10 per cent of the things I buy regularly have an ingredients label and I wouldn't want many of them to have more than a few ingredients. So you want to cut out processed foods (the stuff with ingredients labels) and what you want to eat is:

Carbohydrates

The big diet craze of cutting out carbs completely is crazy and it doesn't work. Your body needs some carbohydrates. So cut down on carbs and avoid any highly refined white breads or pastas, but do eat some good carbs every day.

Protein

Eat lean protein at every meal: chicken, turkey, fish or seafood. Try some alternatives to meat like beans, pulses and nuts. Hummus and nut butters are a great way to add protein to your snacks.

Fruit and veg

Lots of it everyday! Fruit and veg are filled with all the fantastic nutrients your body needs to do its work. Dark leafy veg is best for nutrition. You should always aim to get most of your five a day from vegetables rather than fruit.

Fats

Yes you need to eat fat, but it should be a healthy fat. These include avocados, oily fish and nuts. Limit saturated fat and completely avoid trans fats.

Water

Stay hydrated with water rather than fizzy, sugary or caffeinated drinks. Aim for 2–3 litres of water each day. Flavour your water if you find it boring by adding lime/lemon wedges.

WHAT NOT TO EAT
Processed foods

Try to cook from scratch as much as possible; food you make yourself will have more nutrients than foods with additives.

Sugar

Remember that it's not just the sugar you see that you have to be wary of, but the hidden kinds as well.

Wheat

Try to cut down on the amount of wheat you consume. Why not replace it with spelt or another wheat alternative? If you do choose to eat wheat, remember to always go for the wholegrain variety.

UNLIMITED	GOOD STUFF	LIMIT	AVOID
Vegetables	**Carbs**	Caffeine	Sugar
Leafy green veg	Brown rice	Salt	Artificial
Tomatoes	Quinoa	Potatoes	sweeteners
Broccoli	Millet		Processed foods
Cauliflower	Rice noodles		Trans fats
Kale	Spelt pasta		Low-fat foods
Peppers	Sweet potato		Takeaways
Cucumber	Oats		White things
Celery			such as bread/
Leeks	**Protein**		pasta/rice
Onions	Chicken		Margarine
Asparagus	Turkey		Fried foods
Brussel sprouts	Fish		Confectionary
	Eggs		such as
Berries	Cottage cheese		pastries,
Blueberries	Greek yoghurt		cookies,
Blackberries	Beans and pulses		muffins,
Strawberries	All fruit and veg		biscuits,
Raspberries			donuts, etc.
	Oils and fat		Soft drinks
Water	Coconut oil		Juices (unless
Herbal teas	Olive oil		freshly made)
	Avocado		Wheat*

	Nuts (almonds, cashews, pistachios, brazil nuts, walnuts, pine nuts, hazelnuts, etc.) Seeds (sunflower, sesame, pumpkin, chia, flax) Nut butters (e.g. almond) Oily fish (sardines, mackerel, salmon)		Alcohol*

This list is not exhaustive but it gives you a good indication of what foods you should be including in your diet and what you should be limiting.

* Many people on this plan have continued to eat some wheat, just cutting down their consumption significantly, and also have the odd drink, so you might choose to do that as well if avoiding these completely seems too much.

OTHER TIPS

1. Read labels

This is a key skill (see chapter 4). The most important part to read is the list of ingredients before anything else – the fewer the better. Avoid anything with sugar listed and if there are ingredients you can't pronounce, it's probably not good for you: go for all-natural ingredients.

2. Eat fuel – eat clean

Ninety-five per cent of the things you eat should be things that give you energy, that fuel you. The unhealthy stuff has the opposite effect. Always ask yourself, is this going to fuel me? Is this going to boost my health or is it possibly going to have the opposite effect? This is eating clean. Avoid all the nasty stuff that's going to slow you down and stick to natural wholefoods.

3. Eat regularly
Eat three main meals a day and two snacks. This is really important as it will keep your metabolism going and your blood sugar levels stable. Never EVER skip breakfast.

4. Eat something new
Explore new tastes and new ingredients. Healthy does not have to mean taste free! Get excited about new foods and the fact that you can eat stuff that is absolutely delicious but that's also going to help you lose weight.

5. Chew
The more you chew the better your food tastes and the easier it is to digest, as digestion starts in your mouth.

6. Watch your portions
Just because you're eating healthy things only, doesn't mean you can eat unlimited amounts, so keep on top of this. Instead of measuring, learn to use the hunger scale to know when you've had enough.

7. Stop. Slow down
Sit down to eat, don't watch TV or dine at your desk. Focus on your meal alone.

8. Eat natural foods

Eat only foods that are grown, that are as close to their natural form as possible, and avoid anything manufactured or processed.

9. Simple meals

Try to eat and cook with single-ingredient foods, like using tomatoes rather then using a jar or a pre-made packet of sauce.

10. Balanced plate

Remember balanced meals – half your plate should be filled with vegetables, one-quarter protein and one-quarter healthy carbohydrates.

SAMPLE MENUS

Following are two sample menus using my recipes to give you an example of how you can mix and match meals from the meal planner to come up with a menu plan for the week. When you are devising your plan each week, consider where you will be for lunch and what will be most suitable to bring. Cooking double at dinner is a great idea as it will give you an easy lunch for the next day. These are just samples to give you some inspiration, so do substitute where you need to and you can always use recipes from outside of this book too, as long as they adhere to the guidelines of the plan.

	Breakfast	Lunch	Dinner	Snacks
Monday	Chia seed pudding	Open spelt sandwich	Roast chicken and Mediterranean veg (leave leftovers for lunch tomorrow)	
Tuesday	Fresh muesli	Roast chicken and veg leftovers	Quinoa-stuffed peppers	
Wednesday	Overnight oats (prep night before)	Tuna salad	Bean, lentil and quinoa hotpot (make enough for lunch tomorrow)	Choose 2 snacks daily from the suggestions (see chapter 11)
Thursday	Choice of smoothie	Bean, lentil and quinoa hotpot leftovers	Simple salmon	
Friday	Quinoa and apple porridge	Chicken and avocado salad	Classic Bolognaise with courgette spaghetti	
Saturday	Banana fritters	Simple frittata	Spelt pizza	
Sunday	Blueberry pancakes	Leek and potato soup (make a batch)	Chicken and cashew nut stir-fry with noodles	

	Breakfast	Lunch	Dinner	Snacks
Monday	Yoghurt parfait	Leek and potato soup	Black bean and sweet potato chilli (make enough for lunch tomorrow)	Choose 2 snacks daily from the suggestions (see chapter 11)
Tuesday	Fresh muesli	Black bean and sweet potato chilli leftovers	Roast chicken and Mediterranean veg	
Wednesday	Choice of smoothie	Open spelt sandwich using leftover roast chicken with half a mashed avocado	Baked sea bass	
Thursday	Scrambled eggs with mushrooms	Chicken and avocado salad	Turkey meatballs in tomato sauce	
Friday	Tina's favourite porridge	Egg 'mayonnaise'	Easy Thai green curry	
Saturday	French toast	Tuna salad	Chicken goujons served with sweet potato chips and a side of ratatouille	
Sunday	Eggs Benedict	Carrot and lentil soup (make a batch for the week ahead)	Courgette and avocado spaghetti	

ACTIONS

1. Analyse your food diary so far.

2. Identify what changes you have to make to your diet and life-style. If there are lots of changes needed, prioritise them and start with the most urgent ones.

3. Decide your plan start date and put it in your diary.

4. Plan your menu for the first week, do your shopping and you're ready to go!

7

LIFESTYLE

In this chapter you'll learn:

- The importance of sleep and the role it plays in weight loss.
- How to improve your sleep and cope with a lack of sleep.
- How your diet affects your sleep.
- The role stress plays in your health and weight loss.
- How to deal with stress.
- The role your attitude plays in weight loss.
- How to be positive.

There is more to weight loss and staying healthy than just your diet. Your whole lifestyle plays an important role. More and more research is coming out proving that factors such as stress and lack of sleep can actually prevent you from losing weight. Some researchers go as far as to suggest that getting enough sleep is even more important than what you eat. Exercise and being active are also hugely important lifestyle factors for weight loss and even more important for your general health – so important that we'll talk about this in a separate chapter.

The lifestyle issues I want to address here are sleep, stress and being busy, as well as your attitude and outlook on life, which often determines your lifestyle choices. We'll also talk about alcohol and weekends, as these are lifestyle choices that often hinder my clients' weight loss.

SLEEP AND WEIGHT LOSS

A 2013 study published in the *American Journal of Health Promotion* found that those who maintain a regular sleep routine – going to bed and waking at the same time every day of the week – have a lower percentage of body fat than those whose sleep is irregular. Furthermore, getting less than 6.5 hours of sleep or more than 8.5 hours of sleep was linked with higher body fat, as was poor quality of sleep. Many other studies have had similar results. For example, Dr Siobhan Banks at the University of Pennsylvania School of Medicine took a group of ninety-two healthy adults and found that when sleep was restricted to only 4 hours per night, participants gained 1.5kg during the eleven-day study.

Why this happens is still being investigated. Some researchers say lack of sleep compromises your body's ability to burn fat. It is also believed that lack of sleep can lead to an increase in the hormone ghrelin, which stimulates appetite, because it upsets the body's balance and leads to over-stimulation of this hormone. A Canadian study found levels of ghrelin to be 15 per cent higher in those who had just 5 hours sleep a night, compared with those who slept for 8 hours.

Another important hormone, leptin, which tells us when we've had enough to eat, is also affected by lack of sleep. Your body won't produce as much of this hormone when you haven't had enough sleep.

The combination of these two hormones being out of whack is obviously not good news: not only is your appetite increased but it will also be difficult to tell when you are full.

Another problem with lack of sleep is that you're likely to make bad food choices. Think about when you're really tired. Everything feels like a bit too much of an effort, so you go for whatever is the easiest option – this is rarely the healthiest option! Moreover, you tend to crave foods with fast-releasing energy, such as refined carbs like toast, pastries and pasta – comfort foods. And coffee or tea, lots of coffee or tea, of course. Your metabolism is also going to be a bit sluggish – your whole body is tired, so naturally your metabolism is too. A German study found that when we are sleep deprived we burn 5 per cent fewer calories than normal and, even worse, after a big meal when sleep deprived we actually burn 20 per cent fewer calories than normal.

All this combined spells nothing short of a disaster. And to make things worse, when you're tired you're more likely to spend the evening on the couch than to go out and do some exercise.

Now, if, like me, you have small kids and you work full time, this all sounds very unfair and impossible to do anything about – what's the point in even trying? But do not despair, we can work around this. Knowing the facts will help you prioritise and make better choices and, if nothing else, it will help you cut yourself some slack.

For instance, if you're a new mother with a baby who still wakes up a few times a night and then at 6 a.m. for the day, you might be struggling to lose the baby weight, but now you know why! The last thing you should do is get stressed about it (see next section), just accept the situation for what it is – that for the next while, you're not going to be able to get as much sleep as you need and hence your weight loss will be a bit slower. This is fine. For now, just focus on your health and fuelling your body; that's what you need right now, weight loss will follow.

If you're a bad sleeper, even an insomniac, now's a good time to work on that. Improving your diet will have a hugely positive impact on your sleep. In fact, that's one of the first improvements a lot of our participants notice. Exercise will help as well, so even if you're a bit tired, get out every night for a brisk walk.

There are many other reasons why you should prioritise sleep. Getting a good night's sleep will help you be more productive, as your mind will be clearer and you'll have more energy. Sleeping enough relieves stress, reduces the risk of numerous chronic diseases and improves your memory and cognitive function. You'll most likely be in a better mood too and feel more positive.

How to cope with a lack of sleep

There are times when there's no avoiding it – you just can't get enough sleep. Here are the best ways to stay as energised as possible.

1. Eat well

The foods you usually crave when tired tend to be the worst ones – refined carbs, sugar, caffeine and processed foods. These all provide a quick source of energy and that's why they are so appealing. However, that energy burns out fast and you will end up feeling even more tired than you were before. Eat plenty of fresh foods, vegetables and fruit. A green smoothie is great for energy.

2. Eat regularly

This is really important for keeping your energy levels steady. If you don't eat, you get tired. See chapter 5 for more details on why eating regularly is so important.

3. Drink lots of water

There is nothing like water to give you energy. In fact, often when you feel tired you are just a bit dehydrated. Start your day with a big glass of water with some lemon in it and keep drinking water throughout the day.

4. Exercise

When you are tired the last thing you want to do is anything that requires lots of energy, but a quick exercise session will actually energise you. Even just a walk will do wonders, or you could try an energising yoga class. Exercise will also ensure that you get a good night's sleep and will be well rested for the next day.

5. Get some fresh air

Fresh air is important for many reasons, but when you're tired it's particularly great for giving you energy. It will wake you up. In the morning, step outside for a few minutes or open the window, and throughout the day try to pop outside as often as you can and take a few deep breaths.

How to get a good night's sleep

1. Exercise, be active

You have probably experienced this yourself – you always sleep really well after a good exercise session where you break a sweat. Exercise can be great therapy – it helps you release stress, forget your worries and focus on the moment. Exercise releases endorphins – a feel-good hormone – and helps you relax. Any activity is good; walking or cycling to work is a great way to get active!

2. Get outdoors

What is even better is exercising outdoors in the fresh air, whatever the weather. There is nothing like breathing in fresh air. In general, we don't spend enough time outdoors. Try to get out at lunchtime, in the morning, after work, even if it's just sitting in your garden. Opening your window will also help hugely when you can't get outdoors. You'll not only sleep better but your immune system will get a boost. As all the cells in your body receive more oxygen, your lungs will clear, your metabolism will be boosted and you will feel better, because the more oxygen you take in, the more serotonin (another feel-good hormone) will be released.

3. Improve your sleep environment

I don't know about you, but my bedroom often becomes a dumping ground for stuff, like piles of clothes, laundry, books, water glasses that should go downstairs, random toys (I'm forever carrying toys out of my bedroom), magazines, etc. When I have visitors coming over, things get thrown into the bedroom to make other rooms look tidy. Sometimes I have to move piles of stuff off my bed before going to sleep – of course I'm too tired to organise it all. Is this just me? I hope not!

This kind of environment is not good for sleeping. It is easier to relax and fall asleep in a clean, uncluttered environment. If you don't believe me, try it for yourself. Next weekend, spend one day tidying your bedroom. Put ALL the clutter away (this might give you an excuse to make a trip to the shops to get some new storage solutions), clean and dust properly, change your sheets, open your window to let in some fresh air (you should do this every night for 15 minutes before going to bed), add some fresh flowers, candles, a nice picture on the wall – whatever you fancy. This is your space – think relaxing, calming, a space you'll enjoy spending time in. When you have organised your bedroom once, do a quick tidy up regularly to keep it that way.

4. Switch off

This has been, and continues to be, a real challenge for me. I rarely watch TV but I do love my gadgets and social media. This is probably the worst thing you can do in the evenings. The best way to stop spending half the night in bed browsing on your tablet or smartphone is to not bring them into your bedroom at all. In fact, for me this is the only way. For years I didn't have an alarm clock, so I had to keep my phone near me to use for this purpose. Recently I went out and got myself a proper alarm clock. I got the cheapest, most basic model and it does the job. Now I have no excuse to bring my phone or my iPad into my bedroom. Initially, I had some serious withdrawal symptoms – what if I was missing out on something important? But quite soon I started enjoying the break, especially when I realised how much better I slept and how much more relaxing my mornings were when I didn't check emails and Twitter before I even got out of bed.

Too much TV is just as bad for you – this should be no news to anyone. I'm not completely anti-TV. I think it can be great for switching off, especially when you're stressed. There's nothing like watching a good sitcom and having a laugh to help you relax and forget your worries. However, in general, we watch far too much TV, and many TV shows are very negative. This is not only an issue in sleep quality but also in quality of life – how many people sit on the couch every evening watching other people live their lives on telly (which often aren't real) instead of living their own lives? Imagine if you used all that time to work on yourself; what could you achieve? TV in the bedroom should be a definite no no, or if you do have one in your bedroom, watching TV in bed should be an occasional treat – it's great for sick days, for example (though once you start this plan, you'll probably find you rarely have sick days any more).

There are two problems with gadgets with screens. The first and most obvious one, which I am sure we all can relate to, is that you tend to stay up far later than you should. 'I'll just watch a bit more, I'll just google one more thing, I'll just watch one more episode of this ...' and before you know it, it's 1 a.m. and you have to be up in 5 hours. We've all been there, more than once. These gadgets are addictive.

Less well known is that research has demonstrated that using gadgets with screens within an hour before going to bed leads to sleeplessness and poor-quality sleep, because night-time light exposure suppresses the production of melatonin, which is the hormone in control of sleep and waking cycles. Furthermore, the type of light (blue or short-wavelength light) emitted by televisions, computer screens and mobile devices is the most melatonin-suppressive kind. Moreover, what you watch on TV can keep you up – anything scary, very intense, emotional, or even worse, irritating (think current affairs programmes) is likely to keep your mind racing and you won't be able to fall asleep easily. I'm sure we've all experienced this.

So switch it off. Try it for a week, even just one night. As with anything I say, don't just take it as a fact because I say so, try it and experience it yourself. Have even just couple of nights with no TV or any other screens and observe the difference.

5. Meditate/Be still

I remember years ago attending a meditation for beginners course. While I enjoyed it, I also found it impossibly hard. In every class there was a talk for about half an hour, followed by 30 minutes of meditating. I enjoyed the talks but found the meditation painful. I could not sit still, I would itch everywhere, my knees got sore and I got bored. In hindsight, it was no wonder. I was living in central

London, in a very stressful job and always on the go, rushing all the time, so having to sit still in silence for 30 minutes was just too much – 10 minutes would've been a challenge. Needless to say I didn't keep it up after the course finished and I figured meditation was just something I couldn't do; it was too hard.

A few years later I did a yoga workshop with John Scott, who suggested that we call it sitting in silence, rather than meditation, because that's all it is. And he was right, that's all it is. Meditation sounds so difficult, like a skill to learn, and at the time I thought it was a bit hippy-ish as well, but sitting in silence I can do, it seems so much more accessible. I still can't do it for 30 minutes, but there's no need for that; even 10 minutes once or twice a day makes a huge difference.

The ideal time to sit in silence is in the morning and again in the evening. In the evening it's a nice way to empty your mind, switch off and make a clear break between your day and the evening. All you have to do is find a quiet spot (in your newly decluttered bedroom, maybe), sit comfortably on the floor or in a chair with your spine straight, close your eyes, take a few deep breaths in and out, breathing out all the stress of the day. Continue breathing normally and focus on your breathing as much as you can. You will find that your mind is wandering and this is OK – let your thoughts come and go, acknowledge that they're there but try not to hold on to them; let them go. Sometimes, you find yourself following a thought and that's OK too, but let go of it as soon as you catch yourself doing it. You can start with just 5 minutes, then gradually build to 10 minutes, and if you want to, build up to 30 minutes over time. If you're finding it hard (or boring, because sometimes it can get very boring and 5 minutes can seem like an eternity), put on some gentle music.

> *You should sit in meditation for 20 minutes a day, unless you're too busy; then you should sit for an hour.*
>
> Old Zen saying

6. Music

Music is wonderful for switching off and relaxing, and if meditation is just a bit too much for you at the moment, music can do the same job. Just 10 minutes of relaxing music can help you switch off at night. The music you choose should be relaxing, instrumental music. There are hundreds of albums of 'sleep music' on iTunes and services like Spotify – you can have anything from classical music to nature sounds or Buddhist monks chanting on a Nepalese mountain. There is something for everyone. There are also numerous meditation albums and tracks that lead you through guided relaxation and meditation. Try a few different ones to find one that suits you.

7. Herbal remedies

If all else fails, try a herbal remedy such as valerian or Bach Rescue Remedy. These can be great and are non-addictive and safe to use. Just make sure you go to a good health-food shop and get advice on what best suits your needs. You could also try aromatherapy – lavender is great for most people, though be aware that it can have the opposite effect on some.

Your diet and sleep

Some foods promote a restful slumber while others can cause broken and disturbed sleep. What you want to do at night-time is to avoid overstimulation and promote relaxation, and there are certain foods you should consume or avoid to help with this.

To ensure you get a good night's sleep, you should try not to eat for 2 hours before going to bed. Try to keep your dinner light and easily digestible.

Make sure you are well hydrated – dehydration causes insomnia, so drink at least 2 litres of water per day. However, make sure you don't drink lots before bed, as you don't want to have to get up to go to the toilet in the middle of the night. The key is to drink plenty of water steadily throughout the day.

Foods that contain tryptophan, which is an amino acid, can promote sleep. Tryptophan is needed for the production of both melatonin and serotonin, two hormones that help to induce sleep. Good sources of tryptophan include turkey, almonds, hummus, bananas, eggs, quinoa, chicken, yoghurt, sesame seeds, brown rice, lentils and beans.

Magnesium aids in muscle and nerve relaxation and can also help induce sleep. It will help to prevent muscle cramps and twitches which can make you restless at night-time and which may disrupt your sleep cycle. In addition magnesium helps with the effective production of serotonin, which is vital for a restful night's sleep. Good food sources of magnesium include:

- Bananas – these also contain potassium, which further aids muscle relaxation. Bananas are a good source of vitamin B6, which assists with the conversion of tryptophan into serotonin. This combo makes bananas a perfect food to consume before bedtime.

- Almonds and most nuts are a good source of magnesium. It can also be found in seeds such as sesame, pumpkin and sunflower. Most nuts and seeds contain both magnesium and tryptophan, making them an insomniac's best friend!

- Spinach and other leafy green veg.
- Avocado.
- Spirulina.
- Oat bran.
- Brown rice.

Calcium-rich foods can also aid in promoting sleep, as calcium increases the production of melatonin, which we now know is vital for a healthy sleep cycle. Many foods that contain calcium also contain tryptophan. Great calcium-rich foods include almonds, spinach, sesame seeds, kale, yoghurt and broccoli.

There are a few foods that provide a natural source of melatonin, cherries being the main one. Both fresh cherries and cherry juice are great sources and it is recommended to consume them about an hour before bed to promote sleep. Grapes are another natural source of melatonin but they do not provide as much as cherries. Consuming cherries regularly may assist in developing a good sleep pattern. They also contain both magnesium and potassium.

Some caffeine-free herbal teas may also assist sleep to some extent. Camomile tea is known for its relaxing properties.

The top five sleep-inducing foods:

Bananas

Cherries

Almonds and seeds

Spinach and other leafy veg

Turkey

What not to eat

Anything that acts as a stimulant should be avoided for several hours before you go to bed. Caffeine and sugar are the main culprits here and you should avoid black tea, coffee, energy drinks, soft drinks, chocolate, alcohol and refined carbohydrates.

Many people think that alcohol helps them sleep better, but this is not the case. While you may drift off to sleep quicker after having a few drinks, the quality of that sleep is going to be far from ideal. Alcohol prevents you from entering the deep stage of sleep, so even if you sleep for a significant length of time, the sleep you have won't be restful and you'll find yourself feeling tired the next day.

Energy drinks contain a combination of caffeine and sugar, a lethal combination for preventing a good night's sleep. In fact I don't recommend you consume energy drinks at any time of the day!

TOO BUSY AND STRESSED

These days, you're nobody unless you're incredibly busy and stressed, obviously. Don't get me wrong, I think it's good to be busy and a certain amount of stress can be good for you; it helps you get things done and keeps driving you forward. I certainly can't imagine not being busy. But if you're constantly complaining about how busy you are and if you're not enjoying it and feel you're just too busy to have any fun in life, then something's gotta give.

What is it that's making you so busy? Is this just a temporary thing (in which case it's fine) or is this how your life is always going to be? What are you sacrificing at the moment? For example, are you too busy to exercise or cook proper meals? What are you doing instead? Look at your time use – are you busy because you're not prioritising right? There's a saying I love – it's not about having time, it's about making time. In other words, if something is important to you, you will make time for it. I also think that anyone who has time to watch TV every day is not really that busy. If you're up to speed with what the Kardashians are doing and what's happening in *Coronation Street*, you're not too busy to exercise or prepare good meals.

If you do want to get your priorities right, start by writing down everything you do in an average day and then look at all the things you want to do that you don't have the time to do. Then prioritise everything, the things you do and the things you'd like to do and schedule these in order of priority. Use the DVR on your TV and record your favourite shows to watch later; that way you won't be missing out on anything. Chances are, after a while, you won't even want to watch them anymore. Or you might find ways to combine the two. Why not do some exercises like squats and core exercises while watching your favourite show, for example?

Busy lives can be stressful, causing you to rush from place to place, trying to get everything done. Stress is a huge part of our lives today and it can be debilitating. Last summer I went through a period so stressful that there were times I thought it would kill me. I was separating from my husband, I had very little money to find a new home for my two-year-old and me and, being self-employed, I had no idea how much money, if any, I'd make each month. At the same time my business was going through a tough time. I seemed to make one costly mistake after another. Everything that could go wrong went wrong. At home I had a clingy toddler who didn't want to sleep. I forgot to eat, yet I put on weight. I barely slept.

Long story short, it was absolute hell, but somehow I got

through it and now, if I'm ever feeling stressed, I remind myself of those few months and realise I can get through anything; nothing could be worse than that time and things always work out. During that period I had to learn ways to cope with the stress. I got into reiki and NLP (neuro-linguistic programming) and these really helped me to relax, focus on the good stuff, see some light at the end of the tunnel and learn practical coping skills. Around that time I also started meditating regularly, even if I could only manage a few minutes some days – it's amazing what a few deep breaths can do.

What happens when we get stressed is that everything seems much worse than it actually is; we make a mountain out of a mole-hill in our heads. We always think of the worst-case scenario and focus on that, but it rarely happens, so relax. For example, paying your rent on time becomes a question of life and death. If you don't pay it, everything will fall apart and you'll end up homeless. In real-ity that is very unlikely to happen.

Whatever it is that is stressing you out, it's not the end of the world. You need to know that you're not the only one struggling with stress and also that you can overcome it. What's important is not so much the stress itself – there'll always be stress in life – it is how we react to it and deal with it. There are some great methods for controlling stress, and if you are struggling, I urge you to explore these. Your first step should be to start with the evening routine outlined above to help you relax and make sure you get a good night's sleep.

Stress and weight loss

What does stress have to do with weight loss, you might wonder. A lot. Stress can contribute to weight gain or weight loss – for me it's the former, unfortunately.

Stress is a common reason for comfort eating. When things get really tough, eating something nice can give you a momentary escape from your problems. You feel great for a few minutes and you don't have to think about anything else but OMG how nice is this cake! For that few minutes everything is perfect in your world. Of course, when you do this, you're not really aware that you're doing it. It's only when you stop to analyse your behaviour that you realise it.

Stress also causes changes in the functioning of your endocrine system and hence the hormones your body produces. When stressed, your body prepares for a fight-or-flight response by producing adrenaline as well as corticotropin-releasing hormone (CRH) and cortisol. Cortisol in particular is problematic as the levels stay elevated long after your stress has passed and it stimulates hunger so that the energy consumed during the fight-or-flight phase can be replenished. Your appetite will be increased and you'll eat more because you're hungry – your body thinks you've burned extra calories, though you haven't. The foods you crave when this happens are refined carbs, because these provide a quick energy source.

High levels of cortisol also tend to lead to fat gathering around your abdominal area. It is thought that the fat cells in the stomach are more sensitive to cortisol than any other part of the body, as they contain more cortisol receptors and hence tend to store energy more readily. Research has shown that carrying weight around the middle is one of the most dangerous places for the body to store fat, as it surrounds the major organs of the body and can increase your susceptibility to serious conditions such as diabetes, coronary heart disease and metabolic syndrome.

I hope this helps you understand the role stress plays in your well-being, especially weight, and maybe gives you a new incentive to take control of things. I used to be the biggest stress-head ever – I would stress over the smallest thing – but after last summer, I've learned to control it better. I guess I just had enough of being stressed and finally realised that things will always work out for the best. Making the effort to do that (it was far from easy) is the best thing I've ever done! Of course I still get stressed – I'm only human – but I am now better able to deal with it.

How to deal with stress

1. Exercise

As I said before, try to get out every day. If you're very stressed and anxious, avoid strenuous exercise as this can make it worse in some people. Long walks in the park, by the beach or in a natural setting are great. Yoga is also fantastic.

2. Eat well

This goes without saying and yet this can be the hardest thing to do when you're busy and stressed, as it's the last thing you want to think about. But knowing that what you eat can actually make your stress worse might motivate you to eat better. Avoid sugar, excessive intake of caffeine, diet sodas and other stimulants.

3. Meditate

This can be incredibly hard to do when you're stressed, so I'd recommend putting on some calming music or listening to a meditation album. Do this every evening and every morning. In the mornings it might be easier to do it without music. Sit in silence for 10 minutes before you do anything else and try to completely empty your mind. Breathe.

4. Think positive and visualise

When we're stressed we tend to be totally focused on the problem and we're terrified of it, dreaming up the worst-case scenario and convincing ourselves it's going to happen. Stress is really fear – fear of not being able to make it or of everything going wrong. Change this into a more positive thought; visualise yourself getting through it. Tell yourself, 'Everything that comes my way, I'm able to deal with.' This is really a key in controlling stress. Even if you feel a bit scared, that's fine – know that you are able to do this. Visualise your day going well. Every morning, when you're doing your meditation, sit with your eyes closed and visualise everything going smoothly.

5. Spend time in nature

Go to a park, beach, forest; whatever is near you. Green is good for the soul; nature is vital. I try to go out to the countryside once a week for a few hours, for a walk in the forest, on the beach, up a mountain. We are so lucky in Ireland to never be far from beautiful nature, even if you live in the city centre. And if you can't get outside the city, go to a park. Walk, or just sit and watch the world go by.

6. Spend quality time with your family and friends

Maybe combine this with the above. Once a week, switch everything off, including that little, yet so loud, voice in your head that is stressing and worrying about the future. Take a few hours to focus on nothing but your nearest and dearest, and do something nice together. If you have kids, there's nothing more refreshing and relaxing than spending a few hours with them, absorbed in their world. Kids really help you to focus on the here and now and stop worrying about tomorrow.

7. Look at the situation realistically

Ask yourself, 'What's the worst that could happen?' and 'This time next year, will this matter?' or 'In five years' time, will this matter?' Some things that we spend an awful lot of time stressing and worrying about are relatively small compared with the time we spend stressing over them. For example, I can spend weeks stressing about going to the dentist; I hate the dentist. I spend hours and hours worrying about it and then the actual appointment takes no more than 20 minutes and I walk out thinking it really wasn't that bad. Every time. That's a lot of worrying over a little thing!

8. Break the situation into small pieces

If you're worried about anything big – a project, a bill, anything – break it into smaller steps and it will start looking more doable. Make a plan, write it down. Then stick to the plan and get it done one step at a time.

9. Be in the moment

The things we stress most about are in the future. Many of them are things that might not even happen. When everything gets a bit too much, focus on this moment, right now. Take a few deep breaths. Are you OK right now? Is there something to worry about in this moment, right now? Breathe, and feel that you're OK right now – nothing to stress about. Who knows if tomorrow will even come?

10. Simplify

This is probably the best thing I ever learnt to do but it's also very hard to do. When my life was too busy and chaotic, I gave away my dog. It was hard but it was for the best, not just for me but for the poor pooch too. Something had to change. I also dropped out of my yoga teacher training. Another very hard decision to make, but I had to prioritise, and doing too many things at once is not a good idea. Focus on what's important right now. If your life is really hectic and stressful, if you're just trying to survive, you might want to wait a while before you start a new weight-loss programme. Focus on the things in this chapter first – learning to cope with stress, relaxing and sleeping better – and when you feel you're on top of things, then start your eating plan. Adding another challenge to your life when things are already tough is not a good idea.

NLP exercise for stress relief

If you want to try something a bit different, here's a nice NLP exercise given to me by NLP therapist/life coach Agnes Janowska:

Sit comfortably in a chair with your feet flat on the floor, hands on your lap. Close your eyes, focus on your breathing, and then focus on your forehead and imagine all your stress and anxiety located there. Imagine a rainbow coming from your forehead, going into your belly button. Now imagine that all your stress is going through the rainbow into your belly button where it is digested. Then feel like all the stress is going down through your legs into the ground and sinking in there. Your legs and feet feel heavy. Stay still for a few minutes feeling this and then open your eyes. Can you feel the difference? You should feel light and stress free.

Tina's top stress-busting foods:

1. Magnesium, potassium and calcium are three minerals that play a role in muscle relaxation and nerve contraction. For this

reason they can be deemed anti-stress minerals and may help you to relax and ease your stress levels. Potassium can also help to reduce blood pressure. Raised blood pressure can occur as a consequence of stress. Foods which contain these minerals include bananas, almonds, spinach, kale and other leafy greens, quinoa, avocado and sesame seeds.

2. Some vitamins can help reduce stress, most notably B vitamins and vitamin C. B vitamins are important for energy production and can also help stabilise your mood. Vitamin C acts as an antioxidant and can help to reduce levels of the stress hormone cortisol and combat free radicals that may be produced as a result of stress. Vitamin C is also important for your immune system, which may be compromised if you are experiencing a lot of stress. These vitamins are not stored in the body, so we must consume them on a regular basis. You can find B vitamins in wholegrains, avocado, beans, lentils and vegetables. Vitamin C can be found, for example, in bell peppers, oranges and other citrus fruits, kiwis and blueberries.

3. Carbohydrates can increase the production of serotonin, a hormone that aids relaxation. The key here is to choose the right kind of carbs – avoid the comfort-food carbs that you usually reach for in times of stress. Instead, opt for sweet potatoes, quinoa and oats.

4. High levels of omega 3 in your diet are thought to help control cortisol and adrenaline levels in the body. You can find omega 3 in salmon, flaxseeds, mackerel, sardines and walnuts.

5. Studies have shown that consuming dark chocolate appears to reduce markers of stress in people. Although the exact mecha-

nism is not fully understood, the next time you feel stressed nibble on a square of dark chocolate (minimum 75 per cent cocoa solids). Dark chocolate contains magnesium, which may contribute, and it can also stimulate the release of endorphins, which promote happiness and may reduce stress and anxiety.

6. Asparagus is another food that has been identified as helping to reduce stress and anxiety. This is due to the folic acid it contains which has mood-boosting properties.

7. Turkey is a good source of tryptophan, which helps with the production of serotonin. Serotonin can help to promote calmness and relaxation.

8. Immune-boosting foods are important because stress can compromise your immune system, which will increase your susceptibility to infection, illness and disease. Include the following immune-boosting foods in your diet: garlic, lemons, avocado, sweet potatoes, oily fish, berries and natural yoghurt.

9. You should avoid sugar and refined processed foods that cause your blood sugar levels to rise and fall, resulting in mood swings, food cravings, irritability and low energy levels.

10. Also avoid stimulants such as coffee, energy drinks and alcohol, which interfere with mood and emotions and may lead to anxiety and sleeplessness.

YOUR ATTITUDE

Your attitude, how you view life, can play an important role in weight loss, mainly in terms of motivation and being able to stick to your plan and reach your goals. Is your glass always half full or half empty? Do you see problems everywhere, reasons why something is not going to work? In short, is your outlook mostly positive or negative? Or do you think you're being realistic by not being too positive and preparing for all possible problems instead?

Research has shown that a negative attitude in those on a weight-loss programme leads to a lack of self-control, poor motivation, poor portion control, boredom and generally struggling to stick to a plan. Those with a negative attitude also tend to enjoy criticising their own and others' bodies and weight more.

How do you view others' weight? Do you enjoy checking out the latest gossip on celeb weight loss and gains? Do you spend time talking with your friends about who's put on weight or who's far too skinny? Or are you more likely to admire someone who has transformed their lives?

Being in a positive frame of mind will make everything, including weight loss, seem more possible, as you'll be more focused on success, not failure; you'll see opportunities where others see obstacles and problems, and even when you do see some issues, they won't seem so impossible to overcome. You will be more motivated and inspired; you'll be more determined and better able to deal with setbacks. You'll feel better about yourself and making the right food choices will be easier, as you will want to make positive choices. Happy, positive people tend to have better diets naturally.

Different studies have proven that positive people live longer, perform better at work, handle pressure and challenges better, have better and more successful relationships, have more friends and better health.

How to stay positive

You cannot change the way you see the world overnight but you can start making small changes today, and little by little, you will notice that these little things add up and make a huge difference. Before you know it, you're one of those glass-always-half-full people who just can't stop being happy and positive. Here's what to do to get you started:

1. Start a gratitude diary

Every night, write down five things you are grateful for or five positive things about that day. These can be small things; the point is that you find something to be grateful for every day, no matter how mundane the day or how tough things get. Write down, in particular, things about yourself – what did you do well today?

2. Challenge yourself to go a day without judging

For one day, judge no one and nothing. I remember trying this years ago and on the first day, by the time I got to the bus stop in the morning, I had already judged about a million things; more or less every observation I had made was negative: I got up too late (again), my hair wasn't cooperating, ugh it's too cold, the bus is late again, someone is smoking near me ... When I realised this, it really shocked me that at least half my thoughts were very negative and, what's even worse, a lot of them were about me as I was getting ready for work. I was such a nag!

3. Observe your self-talk

When you try to go a day without judging, you will probably find, like me, that the person you judge most is yourself – how you look in the mirror, what you say, what you should have or shouldn't have done, etc. We do this without even realising it, but it's not good for you. Would you let anyone else talk to you like that? Then why do it yourself? Would you say those things to your friends? Then why do you think you deserve to hear them yourself? Treat yourself with the respect you deserve, the same respect with which you treat others. Only say kind things to yourself.

4. Replace a negative thought with a positive

It's impossible to stop negative thoughts all of a sudden or forever. I doubt there are any people in the world who never think anything negative, except perhaps the Dalai Lama. What you can and should do is start reducing the number of negative thoughts in your head. Next time you have a negative thought, catch yourself quickly and replace it with something positive about the situation, anything, just do it quickly.

5. Avoid the news and gossip media

Sometimes it seems like there is never anything positive in the news. Unfortunately, bad, horrible things happen all the time all around the world, but so do good things. In fact, there is more good in the world than there is bad – we just tend to prefer to talk about the bad. We love drama, whether we like to admit it or not. Stop watching and reading the news; it really does you no favours. Not reading about every horrible thing that happens in the world, every person who has lost their job or is having a hard time, doesn't make you a bad or an uncaring person. You feeling depressed about the news is not going to help anyone, least of all you. If and when something major happens in the world, you will hear about it, so don't worry about missing anything.

Another type of media to avoid is gossip magazines, blogs and websites. These are full of catty comments and criticism of people, usually women, and particularly about their looks or weight. A lot of them seem to be fuelled by jealousy and a need to make people look bad. It is the age-old syndrome of criticising others so you don't have to face your own faults. I often imagine the people who write these nasty gossip pages as bitter people stuck behind their screens feeling miserable, insecure and unhappy with themselves. Stop reading them.

6. Watch uplifting funny movies and sitcoms

There's nothing like a good laugh to put you in a great mood and relieve stress and help you relax. Find a good sitcom to watch – an episode of *Modern Family* helps me to switch off and cheers me up – or a good funny movie to relax with. Avoid depressing, sad or intense movies – these will have the opposite effect.

7. Read positive stories

The world is full of amazing uplifting stories about people who have achieved remarkable things against all the odds, and these people always have the most amazingly positive attitude that we all could learn from. Hearing their stories is guaranteed to get you thinking positively.

8. Avoid negative people

If you have people in your life who always get you feeling really negative or irritated, avoid them. Those people who always point out the negative in anything, the ones who tell you to be realistic, the ones who always want to have a 'healthy debate' or say things like 'I'm just playing devil's advocate here,' and leave you feeling discouraged and exhausted. Your time is limited, so there is no point spending time with people who leave you feeling anything but great. Only you can choose who to spend your time with, so choose wisely and don't worry about appearing selfish.

9. Use affirmations

Affirmations are positive statements you say to yourself repeatedly until you start believing yourself. These can be anything you want. Usually, you would use them to replace negative thoughts and beliefs. So, for example, if you are not feeling confident and are unsure what you're doing, you could tell yourself, 'I am confident. I always know what to do,' or if you're feeling very negative, tell yourself, 'I always see the good in every situation.' A great affirmation for weight loss would be 'I am happy with my weight. I love my body. I am at a healthy weight.' If you say this to yourself repeatedly, numerous times a day for couple of weeks, you will find that your behaviour will change; you will start treating yourself and your body better, eating better, wanting to move more as you start being happier with yourself. In other words, you will start treating your body better because you love it, because you want to look after it, rather than because you hate it. With this change in your motivation, from hating and being unhappy with your body to loving and respecting it, you'll find weight loss, eating right and moving all of a sudden become much more positive and natural experiences.

10. Visualise

Visualisation goes hand in hand with affirmations. We have already used it to set your weight-loss targets and get you focused, but you can also use it to keep yourself in a positive frame of mind. It is great to start your day with a visualisation. Sit down, close your eyes, relax, take a few deep breaths and visualise your day going smoothly – everything goes just perfectly, you are confident and feel positive. In your mind go through any stressful or difficult situations you know you have to face that day and visualise them going exactly the way you want them to go.

With all this positivity, it's also important to point out that while you want to think positive as much as possible, it's also important that you do not suppress negative thoughts and feelings. Negative feelings like anger, jealousy and disappointment are just a part of being human. We all have them – you wouldn't be normal if you didn't. If you deny yourself these feelings, pretend they're not happening, you'll only bottle them up. They are not going to go anywhere until you process and really deal with them – and sooner or later you'll explode. Accept that you have these feelings. Feel them and let them out; that is the only way to get them out of your system. When you've let it out, beaten the pillow, screamed and cried, when you're calm again, ask yourself are you really being realistic? Are things really that bad? Is there anything positive in the situation? Will this matter in few years' time? Think about it realistically and more often than not the situation doesn't seem half as bad as it did before.

In summary, have a look at your life and how you spend your time now. Do you see problems everywhere or opportunities? How stressed are you? Is the stress controlling you? Do you always feel short of time? Do you enjoy being busy? Do you take time out for yourself? Do you always put yourself last? If you're not completely happy with the way things are going, sit down, write down how you use your time, what's stressing you out, and see what changes you can make. Remember to look after yourself first, this is really important. If you don't have the time, you have to make the time. Think how you'll feel in ten years' time when you look back on this period of your life.

SURVIVING WEEKENDS

One of the most common reasons women on our courses are not making progress is due to their actions over the weekend.

Weekends are all about relaxing and recuperating from the stresses of the week. For many people it is a time for some self-indulgence. This may mean taking some time out and getting your nails manicured or spending a couple of hours in the hairdressers, maybe having the joy of a sleep-in without the fear of the alarm clock, or catching up with friends. For many people, though, weekend antics tend to revolve around food and drink. Meeting a friend for coffee and the obligatory scone; birthday dinners and drinks; your usual Friday night out; Sunday lunch with all the trimmings; and succumbing to those hangover munchies.

If you are serious about taking control of your health and weight loss you will have to reconsider the free rein you allow yourself when it comes to food and alcohol intake at the weekends.

Weight loss is all about controlling our food and energy intake through choosing healthy and nutritious food, which will fuel and nourish our bodies – lots of vegetables, lean protein, healthy fats and wholegrains, and complex carbohydrates. This doesn't mean you can never indulge in your old favourite treats again, but it's all about knowing when to stop, controlling yourself and staying focused.

Many people are disciplined and eat well Monday to Friday and assume that because of this they can eat whatever they wish at the weekend. For a lucky few this may very well be the case. These people are usually those already at a healthy weight, who are active and can afford to indulge more than the person who is focusing on fat loss. When it comes to it, weight loss is really about the average food intake over the course of a week, so yes, weekends do count!

Even if you have conscientiously maintained your food and energy intake at a healthy level from Monday to Friday, a weekend blowout can undo all your good efforts – I have seen this over and over again in my groups. Having one treat meal *within reason* at the weekend will not hinder your weight loss once the remainder of the week has been healthy, as it is all about the combined over-all effort. However, if each and every weekend you are eating and drinking without caution, your weight loss will be sabotaged. You might not put on any weight but you can also be certain you won't lose any either.

In terms of science and in relation to energy balance, it is said that in order to lose a pound of body fat a week you must create an energy deficit of 3,500 calories. So that means an average reduction of 500 calories from your diet each day. Think about how you eat over the weekend – your indulgences could easily cost you your calorie deficit, resulting in zero weight loss that week. While we try not to focus on calories too much in our healthy eating plan (there is so much more to food than calories), the amount and type of food you eat is important when it comes to weight loss, which is why it is important to exercise control over portion sizes.

If you consume an additional 500 calories or so at the weekend, this is not going to negatively impact your overall weight loss, as your average intake over the whole week is what matters. If you have made healthy choices during the rest of the week, your average energy intake should still be in a good range even after allowing yourself a small weekend treat. However, if you choose to use the weekend as an excuse to eat and drink excessively, you will bring your average energy intake way up. This can result in your weight loss stalling or perhaps even cause you to put on a pound. Many people can easily consume double or more the number of calories on a Saturday or Sunday than they would during the week.

A big problem with weekend blowouts is that they often tend to involve carbohydrate-rich meals and often of the processed variety – think along the lines of pizza, chips, pasta, bread, crisps and cake. Carbohydrates are stored in the body with 3g of water for every 1g of carbohydrate consumed. This will leave you very bloated and retaining a lot of water. Taking this into consideration, do you think you are going to see any movement on the weighing scales the week after an excessive weekend? Although you may not have necessarily put on any body fat, you will still not see any progression in your weight loss as a consequence of the water retention.

DEALING WITH ALCOHOL

Alcohol is a real diet buster that sabotages your weight loss progression. It contains a lot of calories, and empty calories at that. Alcohol stimulates appetite and, in combination with a weakened resolve, this spells disaster. The damage usually does not end on the night out; the next day is a danger period as well. In addition, any fat burning is put on hold while your body works to metabolise the alcohol you have consumed. This also means that whatever food you consume in that time is more likely to be stored as fat – so, yes, that late-night burger and chips really does go straight to your hips!

One bottle of wine contains on average 550 calories. A pint of beer contains 200 calories on average, and one small bottle of Bulmers 139 calories. How many of these can you knock back in a night? It is so easy to clock up the calories while drinking; the sheer number of calories consumed from alcohol alone is enough to destroy any energy deficit you created during the week.

It should go without saying that alcohol is not recommended as part of any healthy eating plan. However, we all know most people do enjoy a drink or two at the weekend. Follow the tips below to do some damage limitation when it comes to alcohol. Keep your intake as low as possible and limit it to once a week or even better, only special occasions. If you are trying to lose body fat, alcohol should not be a regular part of your diet.

Facts about alcohol and fat loss

- Alcohol contains seven calories per gram and is very high in sugar.

- Our bodies do not have the ability to store alcohol, therefore it must be burned as fuel. This means all the food we consume in the meantime is put on the back burner when it comes to being used as energy and is more likely to be stored as fat.

- Alcohol acts as an appetite stimulant and many people find themselves in the queue for pizza or chips after a night out.

- This usually continues the next day as people feed their hangovers with lots of unhealthy foods and find it hard to resist anything fatty, salty and sugary.

- Alcohol interferes with hormones and can encourage fat deposition, particularly around the stomach area.

What causes a hangover?

The liver detoxifies and removes alcohol from the body. The liver only has the ability to process a small amount of alcohol per hour (about one alcoholic unit/hour), therefore the more you drink, the more alcohol your liver has to process. This leads to a build-up of alcohol in the body and thereby to intoxication.

In the liver alcohol is broken down into acetaldehyde, which is a substance more toxic than alcohol itself. It is the presence of this substance that leads to the symptoms of a hangover such as vomiting, nausea and headaches. Acetaldehyde is further broken down into less harmful substances which are then removed from the body as waste.

Hangovers also result from a number of other factors:

- Alcohol is a diuretic, causing people to urinate more and hence become dehydrated. Dehydration is the main cause of hangovers and manifests in the form of a dry mouth, headache and general lethargy.

- The frequent urination also results in loss of salts and potassium that are necessary for proper nerve and muscle function and can also result in headaches, fatigue and nausea, etc.

- Alcohol can irritate the lining of the stomach and increase the production of acid, leading to an upset stomach and cramps the next day.

- Blood sugar levels can fall steeply when alcohol is consumed, resulting in tiredness, moodiness and shakiness.

- Alcohol can cause the blood vessels to dilate which can lead to headaches.

- Alcohol affects the quality of sleep, and while we often nod off easily after alcohol intake, the quality of sleep which follows is disrupted and far from restful.

- Congeners are substances produced during the fermentation process that are responsible for the taste and aroma in distilled drinks and they also contribute to hangovers. Darker-coloured alcohols in general contain more congeners than clearer drinks.

- Alcohol impairs absorption and enhances excretion of vitamins.

How to handle your drink

The only way to truly avoid a hangover is obviously not to drink! If you do drink, however, here are few tips to help you mitigate the damage done.

Before you drink

- Make sure you eat a substantial meal. Having a full stomach will slow down the rate at which alcohol is absorbed in the body and will also ease the irritation which alcohol causes to the lining of your stomach.

- Ensure you drink plenty of water throughout the day. This will make sure your body is well hydrated before the diuretic effect of alcohol takes hold.

While drinking

- Drink in moderation! If you don't you'll be counting the pounds in both senses of the word (£ and lbs)!

- Have a glass of water between alcoholic drinks. This will help keep you hydrated and also give your body more time to process the alcohol while reducing irritation of the stomach. Just before the bar is about to close or you are about to leave, get a pint of water.

- Be choosy with your drink – darker-coloured drinks generally contain more congeners than clearer alcohols.

- Avoid sugar-laden alcopops and fizzy drinks such as mixers. Such drinks speed up the absorption of alcohol into your bloodstream and the overload of sugar alone is enough to give you that hungover feeling the next day.

After drinking

- Skip the greasy chipper – you will only feel worse in the morning. Your liver is already under pressure trying to metabolise the alcohol you have consumed. Eating high-fat foods will only put it under more stress.

- Water, water, water. Drink a pint or two before you go to bed and make sure you have a glass to hand for when you wake up.

The morning after

- You need to rehydrate. While you may feel like reaching for that can of Coke, it is the last thing you need. The only thing you need to drink is H_2O and lots of it!

- Your liver is worked to the max the day after a heavy drinking session, trying to metabolise all the alcohol you consumed. As a result you may suffer from low blood sugar levels which can result in you feeling irritated and moody. For this reason you need to eat something, even if it is the last thing you feel like doing. Orange juice, which contains fructose, will help bring up your blood sugar levels and has also been shown to help the liver metabolise alcohol.

- If your stomach isn't upset, take some painkillers if you have a headache.

- Have a nap. Sleep after alcohol intake is not the same as a regular sleep and this is one of the reasons you may feel tired and irritable, so don't feel guilty about having a nap the next day.

The best foods to ease a hangover

- **Eggs** contain an amino acid called cysteine, which helps to break down the toxin acetaldehyde. Eggs are also easily digested.

- **Bananas** will help replace some lost electrolytes, potassium and magnesium, and give you a good energy boost. They also contain fructose, which may aid faster metabolism of the alcohol.

- **Ginger tea** can soothe an upset and irritated stomach.

- **Fruit juice** may increase the rate at which the body gets rid of toxins from alcohol according to some studies. It will also replace some lost vitamins.

- **Water** speaks for itself.

- **Carbs** can be good to bring your blood sugar levels back up. Normally your liver can help to control your blood sugar levels, but following intake of alcohol it is busy trying to metabolise the alcohol and your blood sugar levels stay low. Stick to healthy carbs!

- **Peppermint tea** can help ease tension, bloating and stomach aches.

- **Tomatoes** contain both vitamin C and glutathione to help counteract the toxins from alcohol which cause hangovers.

- **Honey** contains potassium and antioxidants as well as fructose to raise your low blood sugar levels.

ACTIONS

1. Make sure you get enough sleep and that your sleep is good quality.

2. Learn to deal with stress better.

3. Observe your food diary – is it full of foods that cause sleep-lessness or make stress worse?

4. Start practising positive thinking.

5. Look at your weekends – do you tend to go off the rails and throw caution to wind when it comes to diet? Look at the ways you can be more organised and in control.

6. Look at your alcohol consumption and aim to cut down. The best thing to do would be to take a few weeks off drinking completely.

8

EXERCISE AND WEIGHT LOSS

In this chapter you'll learn:

- The importance of exercise.

- How to get yourself off the couch.

- Exercises to try.

If you hate exercise and are tempted to skip this chapter, please don't, because I can convince you to change your mind. I have built a career out of showing exercise haters how to learn to enjoy it. Many people hate exercise and the only thing that will ever convince them to do any exercise is the promise of dramatic weight loss. But the kind of exercise you'll have to do for dramatic weight loss to happen is not going to make you fall in love with exercise! In fact, women often see exercise solely as a necessary evil to lose weight or control weight – 90 per cent of the people signing up to one of our Running Made Easy™ courses state 'losing weight' as their main motivator to start running – practically no one really wants to start running just to run. One of our Run with Tina missions, therefore, is to convince people that there are other reasons to run and that sometimes you don't really need any other reason than just wanting to run. Luckily, I've been pretty successful at this, and usually by week four many of the women who train with me have forgotten about the weight loss as they notice all the other benefits and, more importantly, find themselves actually enjoying running. This is pretty amazing when you consider that most of these women would say they have never enjoyed exercise!

There are two things about exercise that I'd like you to think about – that, with the right attitude and approach, you too can enjoy exercise, and that there are other much more important benefits to it than just weight loss.

Remember that while you cannot out-exercise a bad diet, you also can't keep yourself at optimum health without any exercise, so it really should be a part of everyone's lifestyle.

If you've watched some of those extreme weight-loss shows on TV you might think, 'No way am I putting myself through that!' These shows are meant to inspire, but research has shown they actually have the opposite effect. A Canadian study found that shows such as *Biggest Loser* actually put people off exercise. This should be no surprise to anyone who's ever seen the show – people are crying and throwing up. Why would anyone in their right mind want to put themselves through something like that?

Most people who don't exercise tend to have a very negative view of it in my experience – if they had a positive view, surely they would exercise regularly? They might have gone to a boot camp class or a spinning class or done a session with a trainer with the hope of losing weight and found in painful and hard, so they think that's what exercise is – it's painful, it's hard, you have to be really fit to enjoy it, and I'm just not fit enough. This is understandable but, luckily, it's not true. You do not have to be fit; you just have to want to get fit. It does not have to be painful; you just have to start at the right level for you. Remember that small efforts made consistently are what is going to bring the best results for your long-term health and weight loss.

The benefits of exercise

1. Improves sleep.

2. Releases endorphins – relieves depression.

3. Relieves stress.

4. Boosts the immune system.

5. Makes you be and feel strong.

6. Improves your self-esteem.

7. Gets you into the fresh air when you exercise outdoors.

8. Can be a great social thing.

9. Reduces your risk of diseases such as cancer and osteoporosis.

10. Leads to increased productivity in life in general.

Tina's Top Tips for learning to enjoy exercise:

The absolute key to keeping up an exercise routine is learning to enjoy it. For the best health benefits, you should exercise regularly for the rest of your life, not just for the summer!

1. Start where you're at. If where you're at currently is the couch, do not sign up for CrossFit or even a boot camp. That might be a goal, but it's not where you're at now. The easiest thing to start with is walking.

2. Start easy. One of the biggest mistakes people make is that

they take on too much. They go from no exercise at all to exercising six days a week. This is the surest way to fail. If currently you exercise zero days a week and if it's been like this for more than a month, then start with three sessions per week. No more. These should be easy sessions. Once you're in a good routine with three sessions, you can then add an extra session, but I would give it at least two months.

3. Do it with a friend. Exercise can be such a great social thing. You can do it with old friends or you can find new friends through exercise. Having a date with someone is going to make it much harder for you to skip a session and, also, you'll look forward to catching up. If you can't find a friend to go for a walk or a run with you, join one of the many online challenges or forums or a group of people on Twitter. These can be great for motivation and accountability.

4. Set a target. This doesn't have to be a marathon! You could find a charity walk to take part in or a 5km fun run. As long as you have something on the horizon to work towards, it'll keep you going. Remember that this goal has to be achievable.

5. Reward yourself. This is so important. Give yourself credit for your hard work. When you have kept up your routine consistently for a month without once making an excuse to bail out, you deserve a reward. Make it something exercise related, like new shoes, a top, or a watch – anything that you can wear while exercising.

WHERE TO START

1. No exercise

If you've been sitting on the couch for the last couple of years, don't expect yourself to enjoy a hardcore boot camp session. A gentle half-hour walk might be enough for you at this stage but if you do it regularly for the next two months, increasing your speed as you go along, you're going to get much better results than you would from a week at a boot camp. What's more, you're going to enjoy it, and slowly you'll be able to increase the intensity of your walks. Before you know it, you'll be running and loving it.

2. Sporadic exerciser

Maybe you're more active – you do different exercise programmes for a few months, start with a boot camp, the next month spinning and then the gym, but then you fall off the wagon and have a break for a month or two until you find something new and start all over again. The challenge for you is actually to slow down, hold back a bit and make it easier on yourself in order to learn to enjoy it.

Often people who exercise sporadically are impatient and push themselves too much. Have you ever thought about why you keep giving up? If you learn to love exercise you are not going to want to give it up. Getting into a regular routine from this place can be harder than it is for someone who is starting from scratch, because it takes a lot of patience. However, it pays off. If you tend to have a few months of doing nothing, then go out with all guns blazing again, I'd advise you to start with something gentle like walking, with maybe a few short running intervals here and there. Whatever it is, it should be easy. Your heart rate should be raised but you shouldn't be panting – you should be able to carry on a conversation. You should aim to enjoy the actual activity (not just the feeling afterwards or the results) rather than work as hard as you can. This takes a lot of patience, but think long term – in a year's time with this approach you will have made much more progress than you've ever done with your previous approach. As the weeks go on, you can increase the intensity of your exercise and add new activities. You should also aim to be more active throughout the day, not just when exercising. If you're really impatient and just need to push yourself a bit, do one tough class a week and keep your other two sessions easy and enjoyable.

3. Exercise regularly – no results

Many people exercise regularly for years but feel they get no results. If you're one of these people, you need to look at what it is that you actually do. A lot of people, for example, go for a walk daily but they don't push themselves enough for it to really count as exercise. Being active is great, walking is great, but to get the most out of it, for 30 minutes each day, you should do something that raises your heart rate. So next time you go for a walk, walk fast; your breathing should get faster and you should get warm. Find new ways to challenge yourself – walk up a hill, walk on the sand on the beach, even try running from one lamp post to the next one or try a completely new exercise, something fun. Also, if you're always doing cardio (such as walking, running or cycling) add some resistance training to your routine – this is going to make a huge difference.

SUGGESTED WALK/RUN PROGRAMMES

Here are two simple programmes for anyone who needs to get off the couch and get started with a good routine. These programmes are for walking and running. You could do any other exercise, but walking and running are easy, time efficient and low-cost exercises you can do anywhere, any time – all you need is a good pair of shoes, a sports bra and something comfy to wear. Remember that consistency is the key. If you want to get fit, you absolutely must stick to the programme and do three sessions each week, no more, no less. You don't want to do any more because you don't want to take on too much at once. Three times a week is challenging enough for most people. Rest days are also important in order to prevent injuries. Along with this walking/running programme, I would encourage you to do a Pilates class once a week to help you build some core strength and tone up.

BEGINNERS

This is for complete couch potatoes. If you've been stuck on the couch for years, you're carrying a good bit of extra weight and, really, the last thing you want to do is exercise, here's a sample programme for you:

Week 1

Three 30-minute walks at a leisurely pace. The aim this week is just to get you up off the couch, out the door and moving. You do not have to push yourself, or worry about the distance you cover or calories burned. Make sure you have rest days and do not do any more than three sessions.

Another thing you should do this week is slowly start increasing your daily activity level. Walk a bit more here and there, get off the bus one stop earlier, take the stairs, walk to your colleague's desk rather than phoning him, take any excuse to get a few extra steps in.

Continue to increase the level of your activity throughout the next eight weeks. You might get a pedometer and aim for the 10,000 steps per day, which is what an active person takes.

Week 2

Session 1: Walk 10 minutes at your normal easy pace, then for the next 10 minutes speed up to a pace where you get out of breath a little bit, but not so much that you are panting or feel uncomfortable. For the last 10 minutes slow your pace down again. You can keep the faster interval up for a little bit longer if you feel you can. Or, if the 10 minutes feels too much, you can cut it a bit shorter.

Session 2: Walk 5 minutes slowly, then have your timer set at 1-minute intervals for the next 15 minutes – walk 1 minute fast and 1 minute slow. Little by little try to make the fast intervals faster. The last four should be at your top speed. Walk at an easy pace for 10 minutes to cool down.

Session 3: Find a 5km route (if you don't know one, you can use websites such as mapmyrun.com to plan one) and walk this. Do not worry about your pace, but time yourself anyway to set a base time.

Week 3

Repeat week 2 but try to push yourself a little bit more during the fast intervals, and when you do your 5km walk, see if you can do it just a bit faster than last week.

A key skill you need to learn is to listen to your body. Notice when you're pushing yourself too much – if it gets painful or uncomfortable, slow down. Also notice when you are not pushing yourself enough – if your breathing is not getting faster and your heartbeat is not raised, you need to push yourself a bit more. You will learn this through experience, through testing your limits, so don't be afraid to push yourself a little bit more just to find your limit.

Week 4

Session 1: Walk 5 minutes at a normal pace then speed up for 15 minutes and finally cool down for 10 minutes.

Session 2: Walk 5 minutes slowly then fast for 1 minute and slow for 1 minute keeping this up for total of 20 minutes. Finish with a 5-minute slow walk to cool down.

Session 3: Walk your 5km route again, trying to go a bit faster than last time.

Week 5

Now you have been in a regular exercise routine for 1 month – well done! It should have become a habit by now and you probably find that when you don't do your walk, you miss it. Now would also be a good time to reward yourself, provided you've stuck to your programme consistently.

Session 1: Walk 5 minutes at an easy pace to warm up, then speed up for the next 20 minutes and finish with a 5–10-minute slow walk to cool down.

Session 2: 5 minute warm-up walk. Then walk 2 minutes as fast as you can and 1 minute slowly – repeat this for a total of 20 minutes. Try to really push yourself in the fast intervals so that you get properly out of breath.

Session 3: Repeat your 5km route, trying to beat your previous record.

Week 6

Session 1: Walk 5 minutes slowly, then for the next 22 minutes walk fast enough to get your heart rate up but not so fast that you can't carry on a conversation. Cool down with a slow walk for 5 minutes.

Session 2: Do a 5-minute slow walk and then you'll be doing intervals again; this time we'll mix them up a bit: walk fast for 2 minutes – slow 1 minute – fast 3 minutes – slow 2 minutes; repeat this cycle three times and then cool down with a 5-minute slow walk.

Session 3: Walk your 5km route again. You should see your time improving by now. If it's not, you're possibly not pushing yourself enough.

At this stage you might consider adding some extra activity into your routine – a weekly Pilates or yoga class would complement your walking programme nicely. Or you might try some weight training – just make sure you do it with an experienced instructor.

Week 7

Session 1: Walk 5 minutes slowly, 25 minutes fast and 5 minutes slowly.

Session 2: Do a 5-minute warm-up walk, then walk fast for 3 minutes and slow for 1 minute (2 minutes if you feel you need a bit longer to recover). Do this for 25 minutes and then cool down for 5 minutes.

Session 3: Timed 5km walk.

Week 8

Session 1: Walk 5 minutes slowly, 30 minutes fast and 5 minutes slow.

Session 2: 5 minutes slowly, fast 3 minutes – slow 1 minute – fast 4 minutes – slow 2 minutes – fast 5 minutes – slow 2 minutes

– fast 4 minutes – slow 2 minutes – fast 5 minutes – slow for 5 minutes to cool down.

Session 3: Timed 5km walk.

Continue with this programme and when you feel ready for a new challenge, start the ready to run programme.

READY TO RUN?

If you are active – maybe you walk a bit here and there and you feel you're ready to start running (only you know when you're ready for this) – or maybe you're a sporadic exerciser who needs to get into a good routine again, here's what to do.

You will do three sessions per week. Consistency is the key, so do not skip sessions.

Start with a 5-minute warm-up walk and then for the next 30 minutes alternate running and walking. How you measure your intervals is up to you – you can time them but make sure you don't run for more than 1-minute intervals in the first week. You can go by distance making sure you start with short distances, e.g. 'I'll run from this park bench to the next one', no more than about 50 metres, or a more intuitive way is to go by how you feel – stop running when you feel you're starting to get out of breath. This is a great way of tuning in to your body and learning to listen to it. It also works as a great meditation!

After your running, interval walk until your heart rate calms down and you catch your breath, and then run a little again. If you're timing yourself, after a 1-minute interval run, walk for 2 minutes.

Walk for 5 minutes to cool down.

Do this session three times a week, consistently, slowly increasing the time you run for and as the weeks go by you will be amazed by the progress you make. Do not try to increase your running intervals every time you run. For the first four weeks, increase the time you run a little (by 30 seconds to 1 minute) each week and repeat the same session three times. Only ever increase your intervals once you are comfortable with the previous one. If it feels like you're never going to be comfortable with your running intervals, you need to slow down. Run at a walking speed, as slow as you can – there is no such thing as too slow!

In eight to twelve weeks you should be able to run for 30 minutes pretty comfortably, but if it takes you longer, that's fine; it's not a race. As long as you're running and enjoying each session, that's all that matters.

It is important to start slowly and keep your pace down to make it easier on yourself. If you go too fast, you won't be able to keep it up.

Apart from your three running sessions you should do one resistance training session per week. I recommend you start with Pilates which is brilliant for women and in particular runners. It will help you stretch out and strengthen and tone at the same time. After few weeks, it would be good to increase this to twice a week.

Warm up, cool down, stretch

Another important thing to remember when taking up a regime like this is the importance of warming up and cooling down. Before you start, it is important to do a few quick warm-ups to get your body moving, especially if you run or walk in the evenings after a day of sitting down. Start from the top and go through each major joint in your body. Begin by rolling your head from shoulder to shoulder ten times, then roll your shoulders back ten times and forward ten times, pulling your shoulders towards your ears. Circle your hips in each direction ten times. Pull your knees up to your chest ten times. Keeping your feet together and hands on your knees, roll your knees in each direction ten times and, finally, hold on to one knee and do little circles with your ankle ten times in each direction.

After your run or walk, do standing stretches. All you need to do is:

- calf stretch.
- quadriceps stretch.
- hamstring stretch.

These shouldn't take more than 5 minutes, so there's no excuse not to do them!

To stretch your calf, step one foot forward, bending the knee while leaving the other foot back. With your back leg straight, start pushing your heel back. This should give you a nice stretch in your calf.

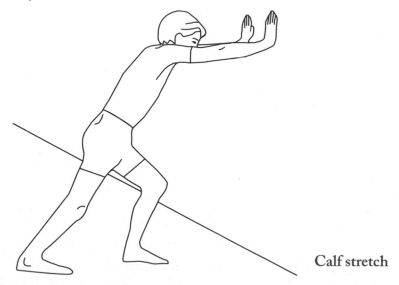

Calf stretch

To stretch your hamstring, stand straight with your feet together, then step your right foot forward with your heel on the floor while bending your left knee slightly; start pushing your bum out, keeping the right leg straight and your torso straight while bending forward just slightly from your hips.

To stretch your quadriceps, stand straight, bend your right knee and take hold of your right ankle behind you. It's important you hold on to the ankle and keep your foot flexed (holding on to your toes, which is what people often do, is going to hurt your knee), and also keep your lower back straight. Imagine your tailbone is pointing towards your heels, to take pressure off your lower back.

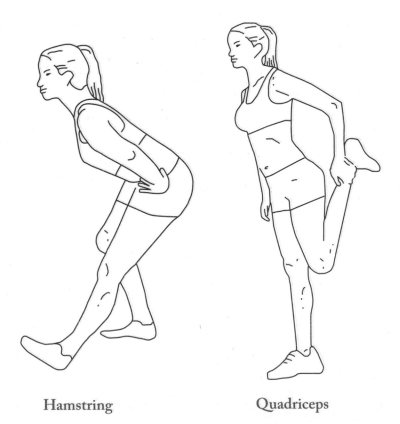

Hamstring   Quadriceps

YOGA

I have a love-hate relationship with yoga. I've practised yoga for a long time and I absolutely love it. But I hate the fact that I see a lot of my clients go to yoga classes and get very bad advice and end up hurting themselves. I often advise my clients to start with Pilates instead of yoga, to build up their core strength, and then try yoga at a later time.

Unless you can find a very good teacher who focuses on the foundation of postures (as opposed to the end goal of making your postures look good) and on how to use your core in different postures, you are better off with Pilates. This is especially important if you want to do a more dynamic style of yoga. Unfortunately, it is very easy to become a yoga teacher (or any other fitness professional for that matter) – all you need is a short course; you can even do a thirty-day intensive course in an exotic location and the entry requirements for these courses are minimal. When you look for a yoga class, check the teacher's background and make sure they have been practising yoga for more than a few years before they became a teacher. Teachers who are qualified in both Pilates and yoga tend to be great. Two great and very safe yoga classes that anyone can benefit from are restorative yoga and yin yoga. These can appear a bit boring at first (for me they sure did), but give them a chance – there is nothing better for relaxation and opening your body. In a restorative yoga class props such as bolsters and belts are used to get you comfortable in different postures, usually lying down, where you can completely relax and let your body and gravity do the job. Yin yoga is a slow-moving class where many simple postures are held for a long time to help open your body more. These classes are particularly great for anyone who is busy and stressed.

PILATES

I used to think that Pilates was boring, something old ladies did; I was far too young, fit and cool for it. How wrong was I! After repeated back injuries (partly caused by bad yoga practice, lack of focus on using my core and lack of focus on proper alignment) I decided to give it a try to fix my back once and for all. I remember my first class – it was a mat class, and I was pretty shocked to discover how tough it actually was. I couldn't believe such small movements were so hard. The best thing was that my back was not sore after it! So I started learning more and did classes with Jett at Pilates Plus Dublin, who is one of the best Pilates mat work teachers in Ireland. I asked Jett to teach me and my Run with Tina instructors simple routines we can use with our clients, and we developed a safe core-strengthening programme, because many of the people with whom we were working had back issues, postural issues or post-natal issues, so they were prone to injury. At some point I discovered reformer Pilates, which is probably one of the most effective classes I've ever taken and also one of the hardest! Now I love Pilates and I can tell you that it's definitely not for little old ladies – although I've seen some amazingly strong and supple older ladies in classes. I've also seen everyone from athletes to models and professional rugby players in the same class!

ACTIONS

1. Start one of the walking or running programmes outlined in this chapter.

2. If you prefer an alternative activity – swimming, cycling, a team sport, the gym – then go for it. Exercise three times a week.

3.   Try a Pilates class or a yoga class.

4.   Increase your activity level throughout the day.

5.   Be consistent.

9

MOTIVATION

In this chapter you'll learn:

- How to motivate yourself and restore your self-belief.

- That you deserve the best.

- How to stay motivated.

'I know exactly what I should and shouldn't do but I just can't do it. I have no motivation.' I hear this weekly, sometimes daily, and I've said it myself many times with many things, not just diet and exercise. We all know the right thing to do, but quite often we don't do it because, well, the wrong thing just seems so much more convenient and tempting right now. This, as I'm sure you know very well, is frustrating!

Before you start a weight-loss programme or any life-transformation programme it's very important to be in the right frame of mind – it is your motivation and attitude that make all the difference. Being motivated will make it easy, but if you're not in the right frame of mind it's going to be a tough uphill battle that is only going to demotivate you long term. When people are not in the right head space, not focused and committed to their goals and week after week get no results, I often suggest they take a few weeks off, because there's nothing more disheartening than trying and not getting anywhere – what's the point in that?

The big question is, how do you get to a place where it's easy to stay focused?

There could be several answers to this; for different people there are differing reasons why they can't get there. For example, they might have other priorities in their life – work, family, caring for someone, for example, or they might not want it enough. Maybe it's just not important enough for them right now. Often, though, people say they want it – over 70 per cent of women say they want to lose weight, according to a recent survey. Many women would say they want nothing as much as they want to be slim, because they know it will make them happy. But if they want it so badly, why don't they just do it? Most would answer with a frustrated 'I just don't know.'

There are two underlying things I've noticed: people don't believe in themselves and their ability to do it and/or they don't believe they deserve it; they lack self-belief and have low self-worth.

SELF-BELIEF AND SELF-WORTH

Most women in this situation have very little faith in themselves and deep inside they don't believe they can do it. Most likely, your track record is there to prove to you that you just can't do it. You've tried one diet after another and failed each time. You've been trying and trying for years, time after time proving to yourself that you just cannot do it. Is it any wonder that you expect yourself to fail again?

So before you even start on any new programme, whether it be this or another programme, you need to restore your self-belief. You need to silence that doubt in your head and replace it with a loud and confident 'I can do this. I am doing this.' How can you achieve this? Well, you can't do it overnight but you can start right now and little by little, day by day, you will find yourself believing in yourself a little bit more.

How to restore your self-belief

1. Use affirmations. Affirmations are positive statements you say to yourself every day repeatedly, good things about yourself. For example, in this situation you could say to yourself one of the following statements:

    I am losing weight.
    I am good at losing weight.
    I can do this.
    I am doing this.
    I find losing weight easy.
    I am completely in control of my eating.

    When you say these to yourself, you have to really believe them, and the more you say them the more you will believe them. Use these affirmations, or any other ones that you feel are relevant to you. Every day say them to yourself repeatedly and when you're in a tricky situation, such as when a cupcake is calling your name, remind yourself of your new positive attitude.

2. Another important thing to do is to lower your expectations and celebrate any small step in the right direction; recognise your small achievements and give credit where credit is due.

    In the past, you've probably been really strict and 100 per cent perfect for a while and then crashed and burned soon after. Failure. You do not want that to happen again. The surest way to failure, and feeling bad about yourself, is setting the bar too high. Right now, what's important for you is to learn to believe in yourself and your ability to do the right thing, rather than getting fast results. Once you've restored that belief in yourself, you'll be able to achieve whatever you set your mind to. You've been wanting and trying to lose the weight for years and years, so you can wait another month, surely? So when you start this plan, you're going to make small changes one at a time and make sure you are happy with the first step before you take the next one.

Start with what seems easy. For example, if you currently don't have breakfast regularly, start with that. Make sure you have breakfast every day. Then, the following week, if you don't have regular healthy snacks, add those in and make sure they're balanced. Once you have your snacks and breakfast sorted, look at what needs to be cut out or changed next. Never make more than two or three changes in a week, all the while making sure that your targets are achievable and you're not setting yourself up for failure. Don't worry about the scales for the first few weeks. Every day you do well, congratulate yourself – you're one day closer to your target and you have done exactly what you said you would do. Every day, write in a journal all the things you did well.

When you feel ready, when you feel that you believe in yourself, that you know you can do this, start being a bit stricter and weigh yourself weekly. Do not set yourself weekly targets – any loss on scales is progress and when you do lose some weight, you should be proud. Also, remember that it is not just the scales you should be focusing on – pay attention to how your clothes fit or take your measurements regularly. Set yourself small targets and when you reach them, reward yourself.

3.   Use your happy weight visualisation daily. See yourself at your

target weight and believe that you can do it. You can feel it! When you can feel it, you will start believing it, slowly but surely.

You are worth it

It is also important to know that you deserve this; you deserve to be slim and happy with your body; you deserve the best in life; you deserve to be healthy. Often people don't believe they deserve the good things in life, for one reason or another. It is usually unconscious and you don't even realise it, but you might often find yourself saying things like, 'Why do I always do this to myself?' when you fail to stick to another diet or fitness regime; it is as if subconsciously you're self-sabotaging. When you do your happy weight visualisation, tell yourself, 'I deserve this. I deserve this body. I deserve to feel this happy about myself all the time. I am worth it,' because you are, you are worth it and you *do* deserve it. Why wouldn't you?

Do not expect a huge change to happen overnight, though once you start working on this, you will notice you're making fast progress. When you get yourself to a place where you believe that you can do it and that you deserve this, you will be raring to go, bursting with motivation! This is great. But it's good to know that while the start feels easy when you're motivated, there will be obstacles. There will be times when you lose your focus and the temptation gets just a bit too much, so you better be prepared to handle those situations.

HOW TO STAY MOTIVATED
1. Live a little, but know when you've lived enough!
As I said in the first chapter, one of the biggest problems with

diets is that they are too strict and that is why they don't work. If you're constantly denying yourself anything you consider nice and restricting yourself, eventually you're going to crash, badly.

Even on this plan, while it's not the strictest, some people still manage to be very strict with themselves on it – sometimes people are so conditioned into thinking that a weight-loss programme has to be strict and tough that they find it hard to let go of this mentality. Whether you find this plan strict or not depends on your attitude – if you focus on the things you're not allowed (i.e. going on a diet as opposed to changing your lifestyle for the better), it will feel very strict. I've noticed, time after time, that those who are the most successful aren't following the plan to a tee 100 per cent of the time. They are really good most of the time, maybe 95 per cent of the time, but every now and then they live a little – they enjoy themselves at that wedding, have pasta on holidays in Italy – most importantly, they do not feel guilty.

Once you've had your fun, get back on the plan immediately. This is the key. Allowing yourself a break here and there ensures that you do not feel like your life is controlled by your diet, like you can't do this and can't do that, and also means that when you do take a break, you still stay focused enough on your goals to know when to stop and get back on track. It is important to know that there is a difference between a lapse and a relapse – a temporary slip up (e.g. one bad meal) versus a series of events that causes you to go back to your old unhealthy ways (e.g. that one bad meal leads to another one, and another one). A little lapse is fine; you do not need to let a lapse turn into a relapse!

If you do struggle to get back on track after taking a little detour, you might need to address your attitude and your relation-ship with food. Remember that you should be able to take it or leave it – you should be able to enjoy a treat without spiralling out of control or feeling guilty. And remember that, ultimately, you should view food as fuel.

2. Be aware of excuses; know when to be tough and when to be nice

There is a fine line between being nice to yourself, allowing yourself a break, and turning into one of those people who always has an excuse, who never takes responsibility – there's always someone or something else to blame for your failings. Say it's your birthday and you want to celebrate – go for it, have fun, have a big meal out (try to make smart choices though), live a little and then next day, get straight back on the plan and stick to it for the next month. There might be another party the following weekend, but you need to stay focused and in control – if you want to achieve your goals, you can't go wild every weekend.

Then there are those people who always have an excuse. When we do weekly weigh-ins in some of our classes, some clients come in every week having lost nothing or maybe even having gained weight. Of course, there is always an excuse – 'It was my birthday.' Fine, one bad week doesn't hurt. Get back on it and come back next week. Next week comes – 'It was my friend's birthday,' the following week – 'I had to go to a work thing all weekend,' etc., and the reason is never them – it is always an external factor, an event, work, a friend. Rarely is it anything more than normal life situations and you just have to learn to manage these.

If you want an excuse, there'll always be one. You need to make a decision: are you going to let these events and people control your diet or are you going to take charge yourself? You might be worried what your friends will say when you're not drinking or eating all the stuff that's on offer. Are you going to let what other people think ruin your diet? Is what people think about you more important than your long-term goal? Or are you just making excuses? Are you just looking for a reason not to stick to the plan? I really don't see what the point in trying is when you don't make any progress. You might as well stop trying, because failing week after week is not going to help your self-belief.

So next time you have a reason to go off plan, think carefully. 'Is this really worth it or am I just looking for an excuse?' If you have a busy social life, you need to choose which occasions are worth sacrificing your progress towards your goal for. Also remember, the better you are now, the sooner you will be at your target weight and able to wear that little black dress you've always dreamed of to the next party.

3. Know that you always have a choice

You always have a choice and your choices always have consequences, long term and short term. Knowing this, for me, really works. Whenever I want to do the wrong thing, I consider the choices I have and what the consequences are. How will I feel tomorrow if I choose this instead of that? How will I feel in six months' time?

For example, it's late at night, you just got home and you had a tough day. You feel crap, you don't have the energy to cook and you really deserve that takeaway pizza. It is *so* tempting. But you really shouldn't; you always do this. Other busy people manage to cook their own dinners and be good. You'll be extra good tomorrow. You'll even go for a run. No one needs to know. What damage can one pizza do? Just this once.

Is this a familiar scenario? We've all been there. If not with the pizza then with something else – chocolate, ice cream, wine. In a situation like this, take a deep breath, sit down and give yourself five minutes to think about it before doing anything. Even better, take a pen and paper and write down your answers to the following questions:

Question 1: How will I feel later this evening if I (a) order a pizza or (b) eat something healthy?

Question 2: How will I feel tomorrow if I (a) order a pizza or (b) eat something healthy?

Your answers will probably be along the lines of:

1(a) If I order a pizza now I will feel stuffed after eating it, I'll feel like a pig and I'll be disgusted with myself for eating the whole pizza and for cheating on my diet again. I probably won't get to sleep easily as I'll be too full and my sleep quality will suffer. I'll feel weak for being unable to resist the temptation again.

1(b) If I go to the effort of making myself something healthy to eat now I will feel great later on, I'll feel really proud of myself for making the right choice and I'll feel nice and light and I'll sleep well.

2(a) If I order a pizza now, tomorrow I'll probably feel tired because I never sleep well after eating something heavy late at night and I'll most likely feel bloated from all the wheat. I'll feel like I have to start my diet again and I'll really regret that pizza. I won't be happy with myself at all and I'll feel like 'here we go again'.

2(b) If I cook something healthy now, I'll feel great tomorrow. I'll be even more proud of myself tomorrow when I realise I won't have to start again and I will have slept well. I won't feel any of the bloating or tiredness I often feel after eating unhealthily. I'll feel great because I'm one day closer to my goal!

Considering your choices rationally like this should make it easier to make the right choice, and when you do make a bad choice, know that you have weighed up your options rationally and you still chose the worse option, so you'd better enjoy it and not feel bad about it.

If neither of the above does the trick for you and you still want the pizza, try thinking about weigh-in day. That pizza will show on the scales.

4. Know that you are in charge

This pretty much summarises the two previous points but it's so important it's worth spelling it out. You, and no one but you, are in charge of what you eat. You might go to a party where there's nothing but deep-fried cheese on offer, but you are the one who makes the decision to eat it or not. It is not the party organiser's responsibility to make you stick to your diet, nor is it her/his fault if you don't. You always have a choice. Not eating what you're offered is not going to offend anyone, if you do it nicely. Don't let anyone or anything else control your weight and well-being, it is your responsibility and, unless you're a small child, no one else can take charge of it.

5. Don't beat yourself up

When you do choose one of the bad options, the worst thing you can do is beat yourself up about it, spend the next day feeling guilty, thinking about how you shouldn't have done that. Do not do this. Guilt never solves anything; in fact, it will only make things worse. This guilt is the reason why so many lapses turn into relapses. You feel bad, so you want to eat something, or you might think, 'What's the point anyway?' and go off the rails completely. It was one bad choice, one bad meal; that's not going to kill anyone and it sure isn't going to ruin your whole diet or make you gain weight, if you leave it at that. Did you enjoy it? No? Well then, remember that next time and you won't make the same bad choice again. Yes? Well that's great – it wasn't completely wasted! Now put it behind you, forgive yourself and move on. It's a new day, get back on the plan, do your happy-weight visualisation, say your affirmations and it's full steam ahead. You are doing great!

6. Focus

Focus on your end goal; keep your eye on the prize; do not let the image of that end result leave your mind. Make it the first thing you think about in the morning – start and end your day with your happy-weight visualisation. Remind yourself of that vision any time during the day when you need it – when you're in a café queue finding it hard to resist the pastries, for example. Use your journal, make vision boards, plan rewards. Whatever it takes, make sure that that vision of you at your happy weight is firmly implanted in your head, so that when things get tough you remember it. If you haven't made it a strong focus, it is easy to forget and be led astray.

7. Make your goals visual

Making things visual always makes them more real. There are many ways of doing this. One really nice way is to get two jars and, say you have 20lbs to lose, put twenty marbles in one jar and one by one, as you lose the weight, move the marbles to the second jar.

Vision boards are a great way of making your goal visual. Take a large piece of paper, have a bunch of magazines and cut out pictures that represent your goal. Glue the pictures on the paper and put this on your wall, in a place where you can see it as often as possible. This will remind you of your goals and help you stay focused on them. There are even apps for doing these now.

If you have a photo of yourself at a weight that you were happy with, or maybe a photo from a magazine of someone else looking slim, happy and healthy, put this on your fridge door.

Money is a great incentive too. Why not put a fiver (or whatever amount you can afford) in a jar every time you lose a pound? If you have 20lbs to lose, by the end you'll have €100 and you can buy yourself something nice to celebrate!

Take before and after photos of yourself. It will take a while for the results to really show in these photos but it's a great way to see your progress and remind yourself where you started.

8. Educate yourself

The more you understand nutrition and health, the easier making the right choices becomes, so make sure you always have something health- and nutrition-related to read to keep you motivated and to remind you why it's so important. Be aware of what you read though, as there is a lot of bad and incorrect information out there – avoid fads, fast weight-loss promises and any diets based on cutting out complete food groups. Go for books and information on basic nutrition based on the same principles as are in this book.

There are several documentaries you can watch on Netflix, such as *Food Inc.* and *Vegucated*, that are eye-opening and will make you reconsider what you eat.

I think education really is the key. It is very hard to eat junk once you know the facts about what it does to your body and health. For most people, though, a regular reminder is needed. You read about it and it makes sense, but it's very easy to slip back into your old habits.

9. Visualise

I know I go on about this a lot but it's such a powerful tool that it is worth mentioning again and again. Visualising is a technique used by all top athletes, business people, performers and many more. It is simple yet powerful. You create a strong mental image of yourself at your goal and you focus on it, feel as if you were there already. Your happy-weight visualisation is a great, powerful exercise to do daily, but you can come up with others as you need them.

You can also use visualisations when you face challenging situations. For example, you're going to a party where there'll be canapés, desserts, the lot, but you want to say no to it all. You are naturally worried how it'll go, whether you'll be strong enough to resist the temptation. That worry alone is putting you at a higher risk of failing. Visualise this event, go through the whole thing in your head and visualise yourself getting through it with ease – with a smile on your face you say 'No, thank you' to all the unhealthy snacks and desserts. You are enjoying yourself, you're having fun and above all, you're feeling great about yourself. One of my clients went to a party with a great big buffet dinner but stayed strong and focused and said no to most of it, only eating a salad. She said afterwards that she had never felt so great about herself. Her old self would have spent the night next to the buffet scoffing everything from the table as fast as she could and ending up feeling stuffed, fat and awful. Now she felt strong and light. Imagine feeling that? Imagine yourself at a party, saying no to all the party foods you usually feel helpless to resist. Feel it. What an amazing feeling.

Maybe evenings are your most difficult times. Visualise these going smoothly and see yourself as that slim happy person. Start your mornings with visualisations. See how your day will go, smoothly, perfectly; you make all the right choices, confidently and happily. You are enjoying your new lifestyle. It sounds so simple but it's so powerful. Try it!

10. Give yourself 60 minutes

When you really, *really* want something but you also know you shouldn't have it, but, oh my God, you want it, and you try to talk yourself out of it and you have this battle going on inside your head, a great thing to try is to tell yourself, 'OK, I'll have it in an hour. If I still want that chocolate bar so badly, I'll have it then, but in the meantime, I'll have some fruit.'

Stop thinking about it for an hour and the chances are, once that hour is up you won't want it anymore.

11. Reward yourself regularly

Rewards are so important. You work hard, so you need to get paid. But often we are too hard on ourselves, especially when it comes to weight loss. We want nothing but perfect, and any rewards can wait until we get to our goal. However, I think it's the small rewards you give yourself on regular basis, weekly or monthly, that are the most important rewards in terms of keeping you motivated and on the right track. Make a list of small, regular rewards you'd like. These should be non-food items, such as a manicure, pedicure, a facial, a new pair of jeans, a bag or magazines. Have some bigger monthly rewards and smaller weekly ones. The small ones are particularly good, I find, because you can use them when needed. For example, if you're having a really bad day and finding it hard to resist temptation, say to yourself, 'If I stay strong all day, I'll buy myself some new make-up at lunchtime tomorrow.'

12. Use social media

Social media is a wonderful way to either connect with people or just get some inspiration. You can team up with a group of virtual friends to keep each other motivated or to achieve a shared goal. Some of my Run with Tina girls have a Facebook group where they commit to running for a total of 90 minutes each week and they share their successes and struggles with the group, which keeps everyone motivated. Sometimes they share photos or even arrange to meet up for a 5km fun run. There are a lot of similar challenges online that you can use. I've used them myself and loved how I could connect with people around the world doing the same challenge.

You can also find lots of inspirational people to follow on all social media channels. People who tweet motivational quotes, post links to great articles and recipes on Facebook, pin inspiring pictures, or share photos and recipes on Instagram. While there is a lot of utter crap and negative stuff on social media, there is also a lot of inspiration to be found if you just choose who to follow wisely.

13. Try new things

One of the problems with diets is that you often get bored of eating the same things all the time and a lot of the foods can be quite boring. Sometimes the problem is that everything is new, so you just don't know where to start, you don't have many recipes and don't know where to find new ones. You need to spend some time every week planning and researching recipes. I try to find one new recipe most weeks. There are a lot of recipes in this book, but after a while, you'll want to explore more. Get a few healthy cookbooks or follow some of the numerous healthy-eating websites, blogs and social media accounts to find great recipes to try and add these to your diet regularly. Explore new foods and new ways of cooking food. Give some vegan recipes a try, for example; you'll be surprised by how tasty and exciting healthy dishes can be.

14. Make it a family affair

Often when women go on a diet, they cook separate meals for themselves and their family, which is a lot of work. Try not to do this. If you're the one who does the cooking, cook these healthy meals for your whole family. All the recipes in this book are suitable for the whole family and they've been tested and approved by many families of Slim with Tina participants (the best feedback on new recipes always is 'Even my husband liked this'), so they are perfectly suitable for your family too. Get your whole family interested in healthy eating and exploring new tastes. If they're reluctant, tell them to give it two weeks and they will all soon feel the benefits!

15. Do not engage in negative talk about other women's bodies

This could go in so many sections of this book – in the introduction, in the positive-thinking segment or in the part on restoring your self-belief. In fact, this could, and probably should, be a whole book on its own, because I really feel this is such an important issue and one that is holding so many women back and putting them in a very negative frame of mind. In the Slim with Tina online groups we have a strict rule – no body bashing, no talking about someone else's body in anything but a positive light. Someone else's body, celebrity or not, is none of your business, just like your body is no one else's business. All that matters is that that person is happy with their weight. What we think about them doesn't really matter, and to even discuss it is a pretty pointless waste of your time and energy. If you always find yourself analysing other people's bodies, ask yourself why. Why do you care? I have yet to meet someone who is 100 per cent happy with their body and who still feels the need to criticise other people's bodies, so if you like to point out that someone's too thin, too big, too muscular, too this or too that, ask yourself, 'Am I really happy with my body? Why am I so unhappy? How can I learn to love my body?'

Also, as I said before, avoid any media that regularly criticises other people's bodies.

16. Accept yourself as you are right now

Very often women say things like 'I'd be happy with my body if I could just lose this stone' or 'If I could just lose this baby belly, I'd be happy.' We put conditions on our acceptance and love of ourselves. We are very good at giving unconditional love to our families, friends and kids, but when it comes to ourselves we often have a number of conditions that have to be met before we can fully love ourselves. You are never going to be perfect. The fact is, when you lose that stone, you'll find something else that is going to have to change before you accept yourself fully, and something else after that. You will never be 100 per cent happy with yourself if you always put conditions on your self-love, so learn to accept yourself the way you are today, with all your imperfections – this is you. Once you do this you will automatically start treating yourself with more respect and looking after yourself better, so eating healthy becomes easy and weight loss will be relatively effortless. You will also start believing in yourself again and believing that you deserve to lose the weight or whatever your goal is. After a while, you will also notice that you never feel the need to criticise anyone else's weight or body; it just doesn't interest you any more. You feel free!

This is by no means meant to be the ultimate guide to getting and staying motivated. You might find that some of the tips above work for you while others don't. Try different things and figure out what works for you – we're all different! Or you might have your own motivational techniques that work for you, so continue using those.

Some of the things in this chapter might have made you realise that a lot of work needs to be done on your confidence or self-belief and that might feel overwhelming. It is always good to speak to a trained therapist to help you get on your feet, so don't hesitate to look for more help if you feel it's too much for you on your own or you're not sure where to start. Alongside traditional counselling, reiki and NLP can be very effective too.

ACTIONS

1. Work on restoring your belief in yourself using the tips in this chapter.

2. Use visualisation every day.

3. Know that you deserve to be happy with your weight and your body.

10

TIPS FOR BUSY PEOPLE

In this chapter you'll learn:

- Simple ideas for prepreparing meals.
- Ideas for healthy snacks.
- Quick and easy meal ideas.
- Tips for eating out.

PLANNING AHEAD

Most people lead hectic lives in a fast-paced world and maintaining a healthy lifestyle has never been more challenging. Daily demands can result in exercise and healthy eating being put on the back burner in favour of the seemingly more convenient, and in most cases, unhealthier choices. However, with the right know-how and attitude you can maintain your busy schedule and still achieve your healthy-eating goals.

The best way to maintain a healthy diet with a jam-packed schedule is to plan ahead. Most people choose junk or pre-prepared food because it is more convenient, but if healthier food is on offer they will choose it. It is time to become savvy with your planning, shopping and time-saving strategies. It is easy when you know how.

- Create a weekly menu, prep ingredients, cook meals in bulk and stock up on snacks.
- Eat your own food. Prepare your meals and snacks the night

before. Stock up with nuts, seeds, yoghurt, raisins, fruit, soup, etc. Not only will you be ensuring you are eating healthily but it will also help you save some pennies too – bonus!

- Do not be tempted to skip breakfast. Even if you are short on time, get up 10 minutes earlier. It does not take long to prepare a healthy breakfast and you will be glad of it later in the day when you are not tempted to reach for the biscuit tin. Breakfast literally does what it says on the tin – it breaks the fast. Eating upon waking can help reduce hunger, irritability, fatigue and stabilise blood sugar levels. Those who skip breakfast may be more likely to suffer from cravings and sugar rushes later in the day. Successful slimmers have been found to have one thing in common – they nearly all consume breakfast!

- Breakfast does not have to be large, cooked or time-consuming. Try some of these strategies to ensure you get in the most important meal of your day:

    o Plan ahead. Take 5–10 minutes before you go to bed and set your table for breakfast; lay out all the utensils you will require.

    o Prepare a smoothie that you can take with you and drink on your commute.

    o Prepare a portable breakfast. Bring a bowl of oats to the office – just add milk and microwave. Yoghurt with granola and fruit is a great option too.

- Batch cooking is an ideal way to save you time later in the week. When cooking dinner, make double the amount and, once cooked, cool one portion and freeze for later in the week. Or when making sauces, such as Bolognaise, or soup, make large amounts and split into portions for freezing to use over the next couple of weeks.

- Remember to always practise portion control. This is an area that many people fall down on, hectic schedule or no hectic schedule.

- Prepare your own lunch. In doing so you know exactly what is in it and when and how it was prepared.

    o   Prepare it the night before – it only takes ten minutes.

    o   Cook an extra portion of your dinner and save it for lunch the following day.

    o   Prepare dinners in bulk and freeze lunch portions.

It may be hard to find time for lunch amidst a hectic schedule but, just like breakfast, it is an important meal that will provide you with energy and keep you concentrated and focused for the afternoon ahead. What you consume for lunch has the potential to energise you or leave you feeling sleepy and sluggish. Some great and quick lunch options include couscous, bean salads, green leafy salads, sardines, salmon and hummus.

- If your place of work has a kitchen area, have an emergency stock in a cupboard or fridge for those days when you are unable to bring your own lunch with you. Great emergency supplies include tins of beans, tuna, sweetcorn, oats, fruit, natural yoghurt, nuts and seeds, wheat-free pitta bread, Ryvita, oat cakes, wheat-free wraps and cottage cheese.

The key, even when pressed for time, is to choose fast, healthy and high-nutrient food over fast, fatty and low-nutrient food. There are plenty of healthy and nutritious foods available which require little or no preparation – fruit, natural yoghurt, salads, tinned fish/sweetcorn, etc.

How to freeze meals

- Only freeze fresh or freshly cooked food.

- Allow food to cool before freezing.

- Label foods with type and date so you are aware of what you have frozen and how long it has been in the freezer.

- Use freezer bags, aluminium foil, plastic boxes or containers.

- Do not fill bags up to the top, as the food will expand slightly when frozen.

- Make sure when reheating that the food is hot the whole way through.

- Reheat in a microwave, oven or on the hob.

- Defrost food overnight in the fridge (some items can be cooked from frozen).

- Eat previously cooked and frozen foods within 24 hours of defrosting.

HEALTHY SNACKING

Invest in several containers to store your snacks each day and to make it easier to carry them about. Prepare your snacks the night before to save time and always plan ahead as much as you can. Think where you are going, what you are doing and what access you will have to food and facilities, e.g. microwave, kettle, etc. Included in the list below are some options for when you need to snack on the go and have to resort to the shop.

- Nut butter, e.g. almond butter, cashew butter, on two oatcakes or Ryvita.

- Tin of tuna or salmon.

- Nut and seed mix, e.g. mix cashew nuts, almonds, walnuts, pumpkin seeds, sunflower seeds, etc., in a container. Packs of nuts or seeds from the supermarket when you are stuck make a great snack choice. About two tablespoons is the perfect amount for snacking.

- A couple of squares of dark chocolate – the higher the percentage of cocoa the better.

- Two celery stalks filled with peanut or almond butter and topped with raisins or dried cranberries.

- Air-popped popcorn – or make your own at home, minus the salt and butter of course. Do it the traditional way as opposed to buying the microwave variety.

- Half an avocado.

- Berry mix with coconut flakes.

- Carrot or celery sticks, pepper slices, sugar snap peas with hummus, guacamole or tzatziki (50g).

- Frozen banana.

- Frozen grapes.

- Apple slices with almond butter.

- A hard-boiled egg and two wholegrain Ryvita.

- Banana sprinkled with cinnamon and a drizzle of honey.

- Natural or Greek yoghurt with berries or chopped fruit and seeds.

- Oatcakes topped with hummus.

- Pre-cooked chicken or turkey.

- Fruit.

- A small salad.

- Two wholegrain Ryvita and a few cherry tomatoes with some cottage cheese or some buffalo mozzarella.

- A small bowl of vegetable soup.

- Pots of porridge oats – most just require you to add water or milk. Avoid any which have added sugar.

- Nākd raw fruit, oat and nut bars – you can get these in all health food shops and most supermarkets. They are made from only nuts and dried fruit. They make a great snack and taste so nice they feel like a treat. (Beware of cereal bars – they are always advertised as healthy but most are full of sugar.)

- Cottage cheese.

- Kale crisps – you can get packs of these in most health food shops and I have spotted them in some supermarkets recently. They make a great healthy alternative to crisps.

QUICK MEALS

If you are tired and have had a long day and cooking is the last thing you feel like doing, it is possible to whip up some healthy and nutritious meals with minimum effort. Here are some examples for inspiration.

Eggs

Eggs are packed full of nutrients and are high in protein, so they will satisfy your hunger. They are also one of the most versatile foods going and require little time and effort to make a complete meal.

- **Scrambled eggs:** whisk up a couple of eggs and serve them scrambled with some grilled mushrooms or tomatoes alongside some Ryvita.

- **Poached eggs:** poach a couple of eggs and plate up with a slice or two of smoked salmon and half an avocado for a protein-packed meal which delivers some healthy fats too. Add some spinach as a side.

- **Omelettes and frittatas:** these are great for using up the leftovers from your fridge. Add any veg – peppers, onions, mushrooms, courgette, spinach etc. – and some meat if you have it. You can basically add any ingredient to your omelette and in less than 10 minutes you will have a healthy and nutritious meal. Serve with a side salad.

- **Boiled eggs:** Another fast and healthy option. Serve with some wholegrain or wheat-free bread.

Salads

Once you have some vegetables in your fridge and a few cupboard staples, it is easy to quickly put together a salad.

- Have a bag of salad leaves in your fridge? Great. Chop up some tomatoes, peppers, cucumbers, etc., and mix together. Add some chicken, turkey or salmon, if you have it, to boost the protein content and make it more substantial.

- **Tuna salad:** Tins of tuna or salmon are always a great addition to your cupboard for those days where cooking seems too much of an effort. Mix the contents of your tin with some salad from your fridge – lettuce, spinach, rocket, peppers, cucumber, avocado, sweetcorn, onions, mushrooms, beetroot, etc. Whatever veg you have will work. A chopped boiled egg works well with tuna. Squeeze some lemon juice over to dress.

- **Chickpea salad:** Again, a great staple to have as a quick go-to for a healthy and nutritious meal. Prepare a salad and mix in your chickpeas for a high-protein meal in minutes. Lemon juice and a drizzle of olive oil makes a tasty and healthy dressing; sprinkle over some chilli flakes for an extra kick.

- **Quinoa salad:** Quinoa cooks quickly and does not require much effort. Once cooked stir into a mixed salad and add some chicken, turkey, salmon or tuna to provide a complete and nutritious meal in approximately 15 minutes. As the quinoa is cooking you can chop and prepare your veg.

Tips for salads: Adding a sprinkle of seeds or nuts will boost the nutrient density of the meal and provide you with some healthy fats. For dressing use healthy options such as lemon juice, olive oil, vinaigrette, balsamic vinegar, natural yoghurt, herbs and spices, or pesto.

Pizza

Take a wholegrain wrap, spread with some tomato purée and top with some slices of buffalo mozzarella, chopped veg and some cooked chicken or turkey, season and place under the grill for a few minutes. Serve with a side salad.

Pasta

Always use wheat-free pasta (spelt pasta is my favourite). Boil your pasta and lightly sauté some vegetables. Once the pasta is cooked, drain and stir in a tin of chopped tomatoes and add your vegetables, mix together and simmer for 10 minutes. It might take slightly longer than some of the other options, but it still requires minimum effort.

Soup

When you make soup, always make an extra portion or two to freeze. This is a handy quick meal when you don't have time to cook. Serve with some Ryvita.

Smoothie

Whizz up a nutritious smoothie containing both fruit and vegetables. You can chop all your ingredients in well under 10 minutes; then all you need to do is blend and enjoy. Here is a great option: a couple of handfuls of spinach, a few stalks of chopped celery, a chopped green apple, some chopped pineapple and a sliced banana. Add a glass of water first and then slowly blend in the other ingredients. For an extra nutrient boost, add a tablespoon of coconut oil and some chia seeds. You can really play around with these and vary your ingredients. This should provide more than one serving as well, so you can have some the next day.

Hummus

Chop up some veg – pepper, carrots, celery, etc. – and serve with a couple of tablespoons of hummus and strips of wholegrain pitta bread. Make a quick side salad as an accompaniment.

Sweet potato

Bake a sweet potato in the oven (zero work involved). Once cooked serve with a few tablespoons of home-made baked beans or cottage cheese.

EATING OUT

Dining out with friends and family is always a fun, enjoyable and sociable situation but when you're on a weight-loss or healthy-eating plan, it can be challenging. Restaurant meals often equate to a day's normal calorie intake and maybe more. This is in addition to the other meals consumed that day. Food eaten outside of the home tends to be higher in calories and contains more fat than home-cooked meals.

It is possible, however, to enjoy an evening being wined and dined without cheating on your diet, once you're prepared and practise moderation. Here are some strategies to follow:

1. Take Control

Your needs being satisfied as a paying customer should be top priority for any eatery, so do not be afraid to ask questions about the food on the menu and to make special requests. People are becoming much more health conscious and nutrition savvy, taking control over the food they put in their body, and restaurant staff are used to special requests.

For example:

- Ask if the sauce is tomato or cream based.

- Ask if the meat is grilled or fried.

- Ask for any sauces and dressings to come on the side.

- If a dish comes with chips, ask for boiled potatoes instead.

- Ask for an extra serving of veg instead of rice, etc.

- Ask for a plain grilled chicken breast or fish served with veg and boiled potatoes, etc.

2. Research

Check the menu on the restaurant website in advance and decide what you are going to order. This will take the stress out of choosing, and you are less likely to spontaneously order a less healthy dish, or order under the pressure of hunger pangs, or throw caution to the wind with an attitude of 'Oh why not go all out and overindulge?' As the old saying goes, 'Fail to prepare, prepare to fail.'

3. Size matters

Do not feel you have to clear your plate when you dine out. Restaurant and takeaway portion sizes are notoriously large and can easily clock up calories and fat. Remember your portion size guide:

- Protein portions should be the size of your palm.

- Starchy carbohydrate portions should be no bigger than your fist.

- Fresh or lightly cooked vegetables can be eaten freely.

Visualise your plate in quarters when your meal is brought out – one-quarter of the plate should be meat/protein, one-quarter rice/pasta, etc. and the remaining two-quarters vegetables. Ask for a doggie bag to bring home with you if the portions are extra big.

4. Pay attention

It's easy to overeat when we are distracted, so pay attention to the food you are eating, savour each bite and you may find that when you are not mindlessly eating you may in fact consume less, as you are giving your body time to register when it is full.

5. Say yes to:

- Fruit-based desserts.

- Grilled, steamed or boiled – the more simply a food is cooked the less processed and healthier it will be.

- Wholegrain options.

- Sharing dessert.

- Sharing dishes. This provides an excellent opportunity to taste various foods, exercise portion control and adds to the social experience of dining out.

- Extra veg.

- Ordering a starter and a side if no mains appear suitable.

- Fruit- and vegetable-based courses when having more than one course, e.g. salad as a starter and/or a fruit-based dessert, and choose only one rich course.

6. Think twice about:

- Going to a meal starving – you are more likely to overeat and choose unhealthy options.

- The bread basket – ask the waiter to remove it if you must. Sip on water while you wait instead. Enjoy the company you are with and you'll find you won't even consider nibbling on bread.

- Dishes with added fats, butter and cream, and the cheese course. Remember, foods that are fried, sautéed or sauced are going to be higher in fat.

- Buffets and all-you-can-eat offers. You may go with the best intentions but it takes a lot of will-power to limit your consumption with so much on offer.

- Supersizing – always avoid this!

- Fizzy drinks – sticking to water will save hundreds of calories and prevent bloating.

What to chose in restaurants
Italian

Contrary to popular belief, the Italians do not merely exist on a diet of pasta and pizza but actually consume a lot of lean meats and vegetables. However, Italian restaurants in Ireland tend to veer more towards the pasta/pizza stereotype. As with everything in life, there are always better options to pick and that's exactly what we are going to outline below.

Pizza

- Opt for a thinner crust over deep-pan varieties and filled-crust options.
- Choose vegetable toppings.
- Swap pepperoni and salami for lean chicken or turkey.
- Ask for low-fat cheese if it's available and ask them to use less than they would normally use.
- Swap chips for a leafy green side salad (hold the dressing).
- Share a pizza with your dining partner and feast on salad to ensure a filling and satisfying meal.

Pasta

- Choose tomato-based and marinara sauces or pesto pastes over higher-fat options such as carbonara, alfredo or cheese-based sauces.
- Choose dishes which contain lean meat and vegetables, in which pasta may not be the main ingredient of the meal.
- Ask for extra vegetables and less pasta.
- Skip the garlic bread. A better alternative would be to nibble on one or two breadsticks instead.

Key words to look out for:

- Marinara, pomodoro: tomato-based sauce.

- Fresco: fresh.

- Primavera: spring-style fresh vegetables and herbs.

Other healthy dishes include:

- Minestrone soup.

- Spinach gnocchi.

- Pasta e fagioli (tomato, pasta and beans in a broth).

- Insalata (salad).

Key words to beware of:

- Alla crema: with cream.

- Alfredo: cream sauce.

- Fritto: fried.

- Parmigiana: parmigiana dishes are usually fried and often contain breadcrumbs.

Chinese

Traditionally the Chinese have exceptionally healthy diets, but Chinese restaurants and takeaways do not represent traditional Chinese food and can be something of a minefield when it comes to healthy eating.

Be aware of portion size when ordering Chinese food. Often dishes meant for one person are big enough for two. A top tip is to use the chopsticks provided – this will help you eat slower and hence make it easier to establish when you are full.

Healthy finds:

- Boiled rice: choosing boiled rice over egg-fried rice can reduce your calorie intake by half. An average portion of boiled rice contains 370 calories compared to 630 calories in a portion of fried rice. Again you may find you are able to share your portion with your dining companion.

- Clear soups and broths are great Chinese starters and won't compromise your healthy-eating plans.

- You can't go too far wrong with steamed chicken and vegetables. Some of the other better chicken options include chop suey or sweet and sour (check the chicken isn't battered and ask for the sauce on the side).

Think twice about:

- Anything deep-fried, such as prawn crackers, dim sum, chicken balls, etc.
- Battered meat or fish.
- Soy sauce – this is very high in sodium.

Indian

Indian food tends to be prepared with clarified butter, fried or sautéed and can be high in fat and calories.

Healthier options:

- Biryanis and dhals (rice- and lentil-based).
- Tomato-, spinach- or cauliflower-based vegetable curries.
- Boiled rice.

- Shashlick (chicken or prawns marinated in tomatoes, onion and peppers, served on a skewer).

- Rice-based dishes such as pilafs or biryanis.

Think twice about:

- Masalas, kormas, passandas – these contain cream.

- Deep-fried samosas, bajiis.

- Lamb curries.

- Pilau (fried rice).

- Poppadoms, chapatis, bajiis, naan bread.

Key words to beware of:

- Ghee – clarified butter.

- Mughlai – cream sauce.

- Puri – deep-fried bread.

Japanese

Japanese restaurants, in comparison to the likes of Chinese or Indian ones, tend to serve food which is lower in fat and smaller in portion size. Many Japanese dishes are stir-fried, grilled, simmered, streamed and braised, which immediately makes them a healthier option than deep-fried alternatives. Dishes are generally meat- or fish-based and combined with lots of veg, accompanied by rice or noodles.

Healthy finds:

- Udon or soba noodles are healthy alternatives to rice.

- Sushi and sashimi (raw fish) are high in protein and low in fat.
- Shabu-shabu – meat, veg and seafood in a broth.
- Miso soup and dashi (fish-based stock).

Key words to look out for:

- Nimono – simmered.
- Yaki – grilled.

Think twice about:

- Breaded and fried dishes.
- Beef teriyaki.
- Soy sauce and fish sauce – these are both high in sodium.

Key words to beware of:

- Tempura – battered and fried.
- Agemono – breaded and fried.
- Katsu – breaded and fried.

ACTIONS

1. Plan your days and make sure you are prepared so you won't be caught out when out and about.

2. When going out for a meal, make smart choices and remember to check the menu online first.

3. Stay focused!

11

RECIPES

ABOUT THE INGREDIENTS

Some of the ingredients in these recipes might be new to you but don't worry – they are generally easy to find and most can be bought in supermarkets, although some you might have to get from a health food shop. Here's a list of ingredients you will need that might be new to you:

Bouillon powder: This is a healthier version of vegetable stock. It generally has a lower salt content and is both gluten and yeast free. It comes in a powder form which I really like because it is easy to use to flavour dishes.

Cinnamon: I have become slightly obsessed with cinnamon lately. There are very few sweet dishes I don't add it to! Feel free to leave it out if you're not as mad about it, but cinnamon is great for anyone who wants to lose weight. It can help to stabilise blood sugar levels, which in turn helps to control the release of insulin. Insulin promotes fat storage, and controlling its release can assist in weight loss. Its blood-sugar-regulatory effects mean cinnamon may also be a beneficial addition to the diets of those with diabetes.

Coconut oil: I rarely use anything but coconut oil for cooking. I love it because a little goes a long way and it has many health benefits. Some people don't like the taste of coconut oil, so you might want to use another type for things like egg dishes (whereas

I absolutely love making scrambled eggs with coconut oil because you can actually taste the coconut in the eggs). I also use coconut oil as a spread and I have a jar in the bathroom to use as body oil, cleanser and hair conditioner. You can also use it as a nappy cream or as shaving cream!

Coconut oil is made up of medium-chain fatty acids, unlike most other fats which consist of long-chain fatty acids. Medium-chain fatty acids are metabolised differently from other fats and are more likely to be used for energy as opposed to being stored as fat in the body. Coconut oil is also thought to increase the body's metabolism, which will further aid weight loss.

Ginger: I use a lot of ginger. I used to like a bit of chilli but I've since realised chilli really doesn't suit me (I've still included it in a few recipes, but feel free to leave it out – I do!), so I use ginger to heat up my food instead. Ginger has a great many health benefits. It has been used as a remedy for travel sickness, morning sickness and general nausea. Ginger is also believed to have anti-inflammatory properties due to compounds called gingerols, and may be beneficial for those suffering with joint and muscle pain. In addition it can aid digestion and can have a decongestant effect.

Nutritional yeast: This is a vegan product made from inactive yeast, which I started using only recently. It is a great source of vitamin B12 and adds a lot of flavour in savoury dishes. Any recipes that use this are fine without it too, if you don't want to buy it. You need to go to a health food shop for this. In addition to its rich vitamin B content, nutritional yeast is also a good source of zinc, folic acid, selenium and is high in protein. Two tablespoons of nutritional yeast provides close to 9g of protein. It has a slightly nutty, cheesy flavour and is a great addition to soups and salads, sprinkled on popcorn or roast vegetables, etc.

Tahini: Tahini is a paste which is made from ground sesame seeds. It contains B vitamins, which are important for energy release from food, and vitamin E, which acts as an important antioxidant. It also provides magnesium, potassium and iron and is a great source of calcium. Who needs dairy for their calcium intake? It is great used as a spread like peanut butter.

Tamari sauce: This is a healthier version of soy sauce. It is lower in salt and is wheat/gluten free. It can be found in the gluten-free or health section of supermarkets.

BREAKFASTS

QUINOA AND APPLE PORRIDGE

Serves 2

100g (½ cup) quinoa

2 tbsp raisins

1 tsp cinnamon

1 tsp vanilla essence

1 apple, chopped

180ml (¾ cup) coconut milk or almond milk (water is OK too)

125ml (½ cup) water

2 tbsp mixed nuts

2 tbsp blueberries, or other berries

2 tbsp natural yoghurt

Place the quinoa, raisins, cinnamon, vanilla essence, apple, half the coconut/almond milk and all the water in a saucepan over a high heat. Cook until the liquid is reduced by about half (about 10 minutes), then cover and simmer until almost all the liquid is absorbed and the quinoa is cooked (another 5 to 10 minutes).

Add the rest of the coconut/almond milk, and heat through, stirring well. Remove from the heat, add the nuts, berries and yoghurt and serve immediately.

MY FAVOURITE PORRIDGE

Serves 1

40g (½ cup) oats

1 cup water

1 tsp coconut oil

1 tsp cinnamon

Handful of fresh blueberries

2 tbsp plain yoghurt

1 tsp maple syrup

Put the oats, water, coconut oil and cinnamon in a large bowl and cook in a microwave for 2½ minutes.

Stir well and add the berries, yoghurt and maple syrup. Stir some more and eat.

Try adding different toppings – seeds, nuts, different berries and fruit.

Tina says: I think the yoghurt really makes a difference as it makes the porridge nice and creamy. Sometimes I put the berries in before cooking and other times after cooking. You could also try chopping in an apple or a pear before cooking.

CHIA SEED PUDDING

Serves 1

3 tbsp whole chia seeds

200ml coconut or almond milk

½ tsp vanilla essence/extract

½ tsp natural sweetener, e.g. honey or maple syrup (optional)

Combine the ingredients in a bowl, stir well for a minute and allow to chill in the fridge overnight.

In the morning, stir well. I like to give it 30 seconds in the microwave.

Top with some fresh fruit or berries and some flaked almonds and enjoy!

Tina says: to make this into a dessert, add 1 tablespoon of raw cacao powder.

YOGHURT PARFAIT

Serves 1

150g natural or Greek yoghurt

2–3 tbsp oats

100g berries

1 tbsp milled flaxseed (milled chia seed will also work)

Combine the yoghurt and oats in a bowl.

Spoon some of the mixture into a glass, followed by some of the berries and the flaxseed.

Repeat the layering process until all the ingredients have been used.

You can prepare this the night before and leave in the fridge overnight to save time in the morning. You can also substitute the oats for some muesli.

BLUEBERRY PANCAKES

(Based on a recipe from http://properfud.wordpress.com/)

Serves 4 (2 pancakes each)

150g (1 cup) gluten-free flour mix
1 tsp baking powder
½ tsp salt
1 egg, beaten
125ml plain yoghurt
165ml water
1 ripe banana, mashed
Handful of fresh blueberries
Coconut oil for frying

Mix the flour, baking powder and salt in a bowl.

Add the egg, yoghurt and water and mix well until smooth.

Add the mashed banana and mix well.

Stir in the blueberries.

Heat a little coconut oil in a medium-hot frying pan.

Using a small scoop, pour some pancake batter into the pan (I use a ¼ cup measure, which is about 4 tablespoons).

When the top starts to bubble, after about 2 minutes, turn over and cook the other side for a minute.

Serve with a tablespoon of plain yoghurt and fresh berries.

Tina says: I use Doves Farm self-raising gluten-free flour mix and leave out the baking powder.

I've found the trick is to make sure you cook the first side well enough before you turn over the pancakes, so wait until the top is bubbly and set before flipping.

These also make great snacks and can be frozen (just put a bit of baking paper between the pancakes to stop them sticking).

FRESH MUESLI

Serves 1

½ tbsp seeds (pumpkin, sunflower, etc.)

½ tbsp chopped nuts (e.g. almonds, walnuts, pecans)

½ tbsp oats

½ tbsp raisins

½ tbsp milled chia seeds or flaxseed

½ tsp cinnamon

3 tbsp plain yoghurt

Fresh berries or chopped fresh fruit

Mix all the dry ingredients together.

Add the yoghurt and fruit and serve.

Tina says: Other things you could add to muesli include shredded coconut, flaked almonds, dried apricots and wheat germ. Mix a big container full of muesli so you have a quick breakfast available any time!

OVERNIGHT OATS

Serves 1

50g (approximately ½ cup) oats
150ml almond milk (or other non-dairy milk)
12 whole almonds
1 tsp cinnamon
Handful of fresh blueberries

Put all the ingredients in an airtight container (or you can use a bowl and cover it with cling film). Mix well and chill in the fridge overnight.

In the morning, eat cold or put in a microwave for 30–60 seconds.

Add some maple syrup to sweeten, if desired.

Tina says: This is a great breakfast to take with you to work when you're in a rush.

BRUNCH

BANANA FRITTERS

Serves 1

1 banana, mashed

1 apple, grated

2 eggs, beaten

½ tsp cinnamon

¼ tsp vanilla essence

½ tsp coconut oil

Mix all the ingredients together (excluding the oil).

Heat the coconut oil in a pan.

Drop spoonfuls of batter into the pan. When one side begins to bubble, flip over and cook the other side until brown.

Serve with plain yoghurt and fresh berries.

FRENCH TOAST WITH BLUEBERRY COMPOTE

Serves 1

For the French toast
1 egg
Dash of cinnamon
½ tsp vanilla essence
1 tsp coconut oil
2 slices per person of white spelt bread

For the blueberry compote
75g (½ cup) frozen blueberries
1 tsp maple syrup

To make the compote:
Put the blueberries in a small saucepan with the maple syrup, bring to the boil and allow to simmer for a few minutes.

To make the toast:
In the meantime, whisk the egg with a splash of water and add the cinnamon and vanilla essence.

Heat the coconut oil in a frying pan on a medium heat.

Coat a slice of bread in the egg mixture and put it in the frying pan. Turn over after about 30–60 seconds, once the egg is lightly browned.

Serve with 1 tablespoon of full-fat natural or Greek yoghurt, the compote and a few chopped walnuts.

SCRAMBLED EGGS WITH MUSHROOMS

Serves 1

1½ tsp coconut oil

3 mushrooms, sliced

2 spring onions, chopped

1 clove garlic, chopped

1 tbsp tamari sauce

2 eggs

2 tbsp almond milk (or other milk)

Heat 1 teaspoon of coconut oil in a wok.

Add the mushrooms, spring onions and garlic. Stir-fry for about 3 minutes, until the mushrooms are browned a bit.

Add the tamari sauce and continue stir-frying for another 2 minutes. Remove from the heat and set aside.

Beat the eggs with the milk.

Put ½ teaspoon of coconut oil in the wok and add the eggs.

Stir continuously until the eggs are well cooked.

Pour the stir-fried vegetables back in and mix well.

Tina says: My favourite brunch is these scrambled eggs with home-made baked beans and guacamole – cooked breakfasts don't have to be unhealthy!

EGGS BENEDICT

Serves 1

2 Portobello mushrooms

2 eggs

Coconut oil

Large handful of spinach

Salt and pepper

2 slices of smoked salmon

Wash the mushrooms and remove the stems. Place them underneath a grill on a medium heat and grill for approximately 6–7 minutes on both sides.

To poach the eggs: In a saucepan, bring some water to the boil. Break your two eggs into two different cups or bowls. Reduce the water to a simmer and then slide the eggs into the water. For a lightly poached egg (runny yolk), poach for 2 minutes; for a slightly harder yolk, poach for 3 minutes; and for a hard yolk, poach for 4 minutes. Once done, remove the eggs with a slotted spoon. Some people find that adding a tablespoon of vinegar to the water helps keep the eggs together better.

Add a little coconut oil to a pan. Once the oil is heated, add the spinach, then lightly sauté for 2–3 minutes until the spinach is wilted.

Layer one slice of salmon on top of each mushroom and top with spinach and an egg.

Season with salt and pepper.

BAKED EGGS IN AVOCADO

Serves 1–2

1 avocado

2 small eggs

Salt, pepper and paprika

Preheat the oven to 180°C.

Slice the avocado in half and scoop out the stone. If the hole is not very deep you may need to scoop out a little more of the flesh so that it will be able to hold the egg without it spilling out.

Place the avocado halves onto a baking dish.

Break an egg directly into each half, no need to whisk. Try to add the yolk first and then allow the white to pour over it.

Bake in the preheated oven for 15–20 minutes until the egg is cooked through.

Season with salt, pepper and paprika.

Tina says: This is a breakfast guaranteed to keep you full all morning due to its healthy fat and protein content.

SMOOTHIES

How to make smoothies:

The best way to get a smooth result is to add the ingredients one at a time and blend each one until smooth. I always start with spinach or any other leafy stuff I'm using, then pour in the liquid (any liquids used in these recipes can be replaced with water), blend that well for about a minute (this may vary depending on your blender), then add the next ingredient, blend, and so on. You might want to add a bit more liquid at the end, depending on how thick you like your smoothie. Most of these recipes make one large serving. Any leftovers can be put in a flask and brought to work with you as a snack.

SWEET GREEN SMOOTHIE

Handful of spinach
300ml water
Juice of 1 lime
Handful of seedless green grapes
1 pear
1 apple
½ avocado

GREEN SUPER SMOOTHIE

Large handful of spinach
250ml (1 cup) soya milk (or other dairy alternative)
1 tbsp Udo's oil (or other healthy oil)
2 tbsp flaxseed
3 tbsp natural plain yoghurt
1 medium banana

STRAWBERRY SMOOTHIE

250ml (1 cup) almond milk

½ tbsp Udo's oil

1 small banana

5 strawberries

25g (¼ cup) oats

½ tbsp ground flaxseed

½ tbsp chia seeds

GREEN SMOOTHIE

Handful of spinach

300ml water

2 celery stalks

1 tsp spirulina (optional)

¼ pineapple (or handful of frozen pineapple)

1 apple

1 small banana

VITAMIN C BOMB

Juice of 2 oranges

2 kiwi fruits, peeled

1 small banana

1 tsp honey

3 strawberries

BERRY POWER SMOOTHIE

200ml almond milk

3 tbsp plain yoghurt

Handful of frozen blueberries

Handful of frozen raspberries

1 small banana (frozen, if you have one)

1 tbsp ground flaxseed

CHIA SEED SMOOTHIE

Handful of spinach

250ml (1 cup) liquid (water or almond milk)

½ cup frozen mixed berries

½ banana

1 tbsp chia seeds

LUNCH RECIPES

SIMPLE ADUKI BEANS

Serves 2

1 tsp coconut oil
1 small onion, chopped
1 clove garlic, chopped
1 tbsp ginger, chopped
½ tsp ground cumin
½ tsp ground coriander
400g tin chopped tomatoes
400g tin aduki beans, drained and rinsed
Juice of ½ lemon
Handful of fresh coriander

Heat the coconut oil in a wok, add the chopped onion and fry until golden.

Add the garlic and ginger and continue to fry for another minute.

Add the cumin and coriander and mix well.

Add the tomatoes and aduki beans. Cover and let simmer for 10 minutes over a low heat.

Add the lemon juice and stir well.

Remove from the heat and add the chopped coriander. Serve on its own, with rice or on a slice of Ryvita.

Tina says: You could use any other beans but I love to use aduki beans because of their many health benefits.

EGG 'MAYONNAISE'

Serves 1

1 egg

½–1 tbsp full-fat plain yoghurt

¼ tsp paprika

¼ tsp coriander seeds

Freshly ground black pepper

Hard boil the egg (for about 12 minutes). Let the egg cool, peel it and then chop and mash with a fork. Add ½ tablespoon of yoghurt and the spices and mix. Add more yoghurt if needed.

Serve on 2 slices of Ryvita or spelt bread.

Tina says: This is one of my favourite quick lunches to make when I'm working from home!

VIETNAMESE SPRING ROLLS

Serves 2–3

50g vermicelli noodles (or thin rice noodles)

1 egg

6 rice paper sheets (square)

¼ cucumber, peeled and cut into thin sticks (remove the seeds)

1 carrot, cut into julienne strips

Unsalted roasted peanuts, coarsely chopped

20g bean sprouts, ends trimmed

Fresh spring onions, cut into 10cm strips lengthways

¼ mango, cut into thin sticks

Fresh mint leaves

Fresh coriander

For the dipping sauce

¼ cup tamari sauce

Juice of ½ lime

1 tbsp rice vinegar

2 cloves garlic, finely chopped

1 tbsp maple syrup

30ml water

Dash of chilli powder or fresh chilli, chopped

Prepare the noodles according to the instructions on the packet.

Fry the egg (on both sides), place on a chopping board, roll it and then cut into thin strips.

Soak 1 rice paper sheet in a bowl of warm water for about 30 seconds or until soft. Make sure you don't soak it for too long or it will tear. Place on a clean work surface or a plate.

Place 2 sticks each of cucumber and carrot on the sheet (towards the bottom, but not right on the edge, as you want to be able to fold the edge over).

Add a little of the noodles, peanuts, bean sprouts, spring onions, egg and mango. Top with 1 or 2 mint leaves and a sprig of coriander.

Roll up carefully but firmly to enclose the filling.

If the rice paper tears or if the roll is very loose, you can take another sheet of rice paper, place the spring roll on it and roll up again.

Cut the roll in half and tidy the ends.

It is best to serve these fresh, as soon after making them as possible, as the rice paper tends to get quite dry after a few hours.

Mix all the dipping sauce ingredients together. Taste and adjust according to your own taste preferences.

Tina says: These don't look like much but are so tasty – the fresh herbs really make them! If possible, use organic vegetables for the best taste.

HOME-MADE BAKED BEANS

Serves 2–3

1 tbsp olive oil
1 medium onion, chopped
1 clove garlic, chopped
400g tin chopped tomatoes
1 tsp ground cumin
½ tsp ground nutmeg
400g tin haricot beans, drained
Salt and pepper

Heat the olive oil in a saucepan and cook the onion and garlic for few minutes until golden.

Add the tomatoes, cumin and nutmeg and cook for a few minutes.

Remove from the heat and, using a hand blender, blend until smooth (you can skip this step if you prefer it chunky).

Add the beans, and salt and pepper to season. Mix well and simmer for another 15 minutes.

Tina says: Make a big pot of this and freeze in portions.

SIMPLE FRITTATA

Serves 1

1 tsp coconut oil
¼ pepper, chopped
½ courgette, chopped
1 red onion, chopped
2 eggs
Salt and pepper
Handful of spinach
100g cooked chicken, cut in bite-size pieces

Heat the coconut oil in a pan on a medium heat. Add the pepper, courgette and red onion and stir-fry for about 3 minutes.

In a bowl, lightly whisk the eggs and season with salt and pepper.

Pour the egg mixture into the pan, mix and add the spinach and chicken.

Cook until the frittata is firm and then place under a grill to cook the top for about 5 minutes.

Tina says: For dinner time, you could add in more fillings such as mushrooms, tomatoes, broccoli, grated carrot, etc., and serve with mashed sweet potato and a green salad.

OPEN SPELT SANDWICH

Take two slices of spelt bread (see p. 318).

Top with any of the following and serve with a large side salad:

- Half a mashed avocado topped with slices of chicken or turkey.

- Hummus.

- Smoked salmon (try the smoked salmon on top of hummus).

- Scrambled or hard-boiled egg.

- Home-made baked beans.

- Turkey meatballs (use leftovers from dinner).

- Guacamole.

- Cherry tomatoes and sliced buffalo mozzarella.

- Egg 'mayonnaise' (see recipe on page 255).

SOUP RECIPES

VEGETABLE SOUP

Serves 2–3 people

½ tbsp coconut oil

1 onion, chopped

1 leek, sliced

2 potatoes, chopped

1 litre vegetable stock

2 carrots, chopped

1 parsnip, chopped

2 sticks of celery, chopped

Salt and pepper

Heat the coconut oil in a big pot over a high heat. Add the onion and leek and stir-fry for 2 minutes.

Reduce the heat and add the potatoes. Cover and leave for around 5 minutes, stirring every minute or so.

Pour in the vegetable stock and add the rest of the vegetables. Bring to the boil and then reduce to a simmer.

Simmer for about 30–40 minutes, checking regularly. Then season with salt and pepper and remove from the heat.

Allow to cool for a bit and then blend until you get a nice smooth consistency.

Tina says: I always use a hand blender for soups. It is handy as you can blend it in the saucepan. I have a cheap €20 one that does the job perfectly!

TOMATO AND BEAN SOUP

Serves 4

1 tbsp olive oil

1 onion, chopped

2 cloves garlic, chopped

2 x 400g tins chopped tomatoes

400ml vegetable stock

1 tsp oregano

2 tsp basil

2 tbsp tomato purée

Freshly ground pepper

400g tin cannellini beans

Heat the olive oil in a large pan, add the onion and fry for 3–5 minutes, until golden. Add the garlic and fry for another minute.

Add the rest of the ingredients, except the beans.

Bring to the boil, cover and simmer for about 20 minutes.

Remove from the heat, let cool a little and then blend using a hand blender.

Add the beans and bring back to the boil.

Let it simmer for another 5 minutes, then serve.

Tina says: I love this soup with a spoonful of cottage cheese stirred in. You could also add a little bit of wholegrain pasta to make it more filling.

CARROT AND LENTIL SOUP

Serves 4

½ tbsp coconut oil

1 onion, chopped

2 tsp cumin seeds

600g carrots, finely chopped

140g split red lentils, rinsed

½ tsp ground coriander

1 litre vegetable stock

Handful of fresh coriander

Heat a large saucepan to a medium heat and heat the coconut oil.

Add the onion and fry for 2 minutes.

Add the cumin seeds and continue frying for another 3 minutes.

Add the carrots, lentils, ground coriander and stock. Bring to the boil, cover and let simmer for 20–25 minutes until the lentils have swollen and softened and the carrots are soft.

Remove from the heat and add the fresh coriander.

Let the soup cool down and then, using a hand blender, blend until smooth.

Season with freshly ground pepper and serve with some seeds or a tablespoon of cottage cheese stirred in.

Tina says: This is such a lovely warming soup in the wintertime. It's one of my favourites. I often make a huge pot of this and freeze it in portions. I use zip lock bags for freezing to save space in the freezer.

LEEK AND POTATO SOUP

Serves 4

1 tsp coconut oil
2 leeks, chopped
Half a small onion, finely chopped
1 garlic clove, finely chopped
250g potatoes, chopped
1 litre vegetable stock
Salt and pepper

Melt the coconut oil in a large, heavy pot over a medium heat. Add the leeks, onion and garlic, and sauté for about 10 minutes until soft.

Add the potatoes and vegetable stock and bring to the boil.

Reduce the heat and simmer for about 20 minutes, until the potatoes are tender.

Blend the soup until smooth.

Season to taste.

SALADS

TUNA SALAD

Serves 1

160g tin tuna
¼ cucumber, chopped
2 stalks celery, chopped
1 spring onion, chopped
100g natural or Greek yoghurt
120g salad leaves – spinach, rocket and lettuce
½ avocado, sliced
1 tbsp balsamic vinegar
½ tbsp cashew or pine nuts

In a bowl mix together the tuna with the cucumber, celery, spring onion and natural yoghurt.

Place your salad leaves on a plate, followed by the sliced avocado. Drizzle with the balsamic vinegar and place the tuna mixture on top. Sprinkle with the nuts and serve.

CHICKEN AND AVOCADO SALAD

Serves 1

120g mixed salad leaves – spinach, lettuce, rocket, etc.

½ avocado, sliced

150g grilled chicken, chopped

1 tbsp natural yoghurt

1 tsp pine nuts

Make a bed of salad leaves and add the avocado, followed by the chicken. Drizzle the yoghurt on top as a dressing and sprinkle with the pine nuts.

You can add other vegetables to this salad, e.g. chopped pepper, cucumber or cherry tomatoes.

QUICK CHICKPEA SALAD

Serves 2

400g tin chickpeas, drained

1 avocado, chopped

8 cherry tomatoes, quartered

1 small red onion, finely chopped

Handful of baby spinach leaves

Small handful of fresh coriander

Freshly ground pepper

1 tbsp apple cider vinegar (or lemon juice)

1 tbsp olive oil

Mix all the dry ingredients in a bowl.

In a separate bowl, mix the vinegar (or lemon juice) and olive oil. Pour over the salad and mix well.

Tina says: This is a great salad to make when you're in a hurry. You can use different beans, e.g. a tin of mixed beans is really nice.

QUINOA SALAD

Serves 1

35g (¼ cup) quinoa
1 small courgette
1 tbsp apple cider vinegar
2 tsp olive oil
5 cherry tomatoes, quartered
2 spring onions, finely chopped
½ avocado, cut into cubes
50g (about ¼ ball) buffalo mozzarella, cut into cubes
A few basil leaves, torn

Rinse the quinoa well and cook following the pack instructions (it usually takes about 20 minutes), then drain and rinse under cold water. Drain again.

Cut the ends off the courgette and slice into ribbons using a vegetable peeler (or a spiraliser, if you have one). Whisk together the vinegar and olive oil.

Put the rest of the ingredients and the quinoa in a large bowl, then pour over the dressing and toss everything together.

SWEET POTATO AND POMEGRANATE SALAD

Serves 4

4 medium sweet potatoes (approximately 400g), washed well

2 red onions

Olive oil

Balsamic vinegar

Bag of mixed salad leaves – spinach, watercress, rocket, etc.

1 pomegranate

8 cherry tomatoes, cut into quarters

1 red pepper, sliced

50g pine nuts

1 lemon

100g feta

Preheat the oven to 180°C.

Chop the sweet potatoes and red onions into chunks and add to a roasting dish with some olive oil and balsamic vinegar. Toss the vegetables in the oil and vinegar to make sure they are coated. Cook in the oven for approximately 30–40 minutes.

Prepare the bowl of salad leaves and add in the pomegranate seeds, cherry tomatoes and pepper. Add the roasted sweet potato and red onion, sprinkle with the nuts and squeeze the juice of the lemon over everything as a dressing.

Finally, crumble the feta on top and serve.

SIDE DISHES

GUACAMOLE

Serves 2

1 avocado, peeled and stoned
½ tsp paprika
½ tsp cumin
Juice of ½ lime (or lemon)
¼ red pepper, finely chopped
1 spring onion, chopped
1 tbsp pine nuts
Small handful of chopped fresh coriander

Put the avocado, spices and lime (or lemon) juice in a bowl and mash with a fork or blend with a hand blender until smooth.

Mix in the rest of the ingredients.

Have as a dip with crackers or vegetable sticks, or as a side with scrambled eggs or grilled chicken.

HUMMUS

Serves 4

400g tin cannellini beans
Juice of ½–1 lemon
1 tsp ground cumin
2 tbsp tahini
4 tbsp water
1 tbsp extra virgin olive oil
1 tsp paprika
½ tsp salt

Put all the ingredients in a blender and blend until smooth.

Start with the juice of just half a lemon; add more if desired – it depends on how lemony you like it.

Tina says: You could also add 1–2 cloves of garlic. I leave this out as it makes it too spicy for my daughter's liking. Hummus is traditionally made with chickpeas, but I prefer the texture of cannellini beans.

STIR-FRIED KALE

Serves 1

1 tsp coconut oil
1 clove garlic, finely chopped
1 tsp fresh ginger, finely chopped
Large handful of kale, torn and stalks removed
2 tbsp tamari sauce

½ tbsp rice vinegar

½ tbsp nutritional yeast (optional)

Heat the coconut oil in a pan, then add the garlic and ginger. Stir-fry for about a minute.

Add the kale and cook until wilted.

Add the tamari sauce and rice vinegar. Continue stir-frying for another couple of minutes until the kale is well cooked.

Add the nutritional yeast, stir well and remove from the heat.

Tina says: This goes nicely with fish and sweet potatoes. I also often make this as a snack.

CAULIFLOWER MASH

Serves 2–3

2 medium heads cauliflower

2 tbsp olive oil or butter

Sprinkle of sea salt

Steam the cauliflower until tender.

Purée in a food processor until creamy, then add the olive oil or butter and salt and blitz.

Reheat in a dish in the oven for about 15 minutes at 180°C, or alternatively microwave for a few minutes, then serve.

ROASTED VEGETABLES

Serves 3–4

4 carrots, peeled and roughly chopped
1 beetroot, peeled and roughly chopped
1 large leek, chopped
2 parsnips, peeled and roughly chopped
1 fennel bulb, peeled and roughly chopped
2 tbsp coconut oil
2 tsp fennel seeds
Freshly ground pepper

Preheat the oven to 180°C.

Put the prepared vegetables in a large ovenproof dish.

Melt the coconut oil and mix with the fennel seeds and pepper.

Pour the oil over the vegetables and mix well until all the vegetables are covered with the oil.

Roast for about 50 minutes.

Tina says: I always put the leftovers in my salad the next day or sometimes have them as a snack. If you find fennel too strong (I love the taste) you can leave it out.

COURGETTE SPAGHETTI

Serves 1

1 medium courgette

Cut the ends off the courgette.

Use a vegetable peeler to shave long 'ribbons' of 'spaghetti' off the courgette.

Serve cold or toss in a teaspoon of coconut oil in a hot pan for a couple of minutes. Season lightly with salt and pepper.

One medium courgette will provide enough spaghetti for one person.

Tina says: You won't believe how good this is! I was never a fan of courgettes until I tried this. You can also use courgettes as lasagne sheets – just slice them finely lengthways.

STIR-FRIED LEEKS

Serves 2

½ tbsp coconut oil

1 large leek, sliced

½ tbsp rice vinegar

1 tbsp tamari sauce

1 clove garlic, finely chopped

1 tbsp sesame seeds

Heat the coconut oil in a wok. Add the leek and stir-fry for about 2 minutes until it is cooked through. Add the rest of the ingredients and cook for another 2 minutes.

Tina says: I love this with grilled salmon.

ROAST CAULIFLOWER

Serves 4

1 large cauliflower, separated into florets

1–2 tbsp olive oil

Salt and pepper

Mix the cauliflower with the olive oil in a large bowl. Season with salt and pepper.

Roast in a preheated oven at 200°C for about 20–25 minutes until the cauliflower is lightly browned.

Tina says: This is also great with chopped or minced garlic mixed in with the cauliflower and oil.

RATATOUILLE

Serves 4

4 small courgettes

2 aubergines

2 small onions

2 large peppers

2 tbsp olive oil

2–3 cloves garlic

2 x 400g tins chopped tomatoes

Salt and pepper

1 tbsp balsamic vinegar (optional)

2–3 tbsp fresh basil or dried herbs, chopped

Chop up the vegetables.

Heat the olive oil in a pan and add the garlic and the onions.

After a few minutes add the courgette, aubergine and peppers and cook for a further couple of minutes.

Add the tomatoes, season with salt and pepper and allow to simmer for 10 minutes. You can add a tablespoon of balsamic vinegar at this point if you wish.

Add the basil or herbs and simmer for a further 5–10 minutes.

Tina says: I love this with chicken or fish.

SWEET POTATO CAKES/HASH BROWNS

Serves 4

300g sweet potato, peeled, washed and grated
2 eggs
Pinch of salt and pepper
½ tsp chilli flakes (optional)
½ tbsp coconut oil

Mix all the ingredients (except the oil) together in a bowl.

Heat a little bit of coconut oil in a pan over a medium heat.

Divide the mixture into four portions and cook for 5–7 minutes each side or until golden and crispy.

Tina says: You can try other root vegetables or a mixture of different vegetables.

SWEET POTATO CHIPS

Serves 1

1 medium-sized sweet potato
1 tbsp coconut oil

Preheat the oven to 200°C.

Cut the sweet potato into thin chips.

Put the chips on a baking tray, rub the coconut oil into the chips with your hands and cook for 30–40 minutes.

Tina says: These are amazing. They go with everything and are also great as a snack on their own. They even satisfy a sweet tooth!

MAIN MEALS

ROAST CHICKEN AND MEDITERRANEAN VEGETABLES

Serves 3–4

1 whole medium chicken (about 1½ kg)

Olive oil

Salt and pepper

1 red pepper, chopped

1 green pepper, chopped

1 courgette, chopped

2 large red onions, chopped

8 mushrooms

1 large sweet potato, chopped

Brush the chicken with some olive oil and season to taste.

Place on a tray in an oven preheated to 180°C.

Roast for about 40 minutes, then take out and scatter all the vegetables and sweet potato around the chicken, add more seasoning and a small drizzle of oil.

Place back in the oven until the chicken is cooked through – this should take another 50 minutes. To check that the chicken is well cooked, pierce it with a skewer or a knife – the juices should run clear.

Tina says: When buying chicken, or any other meat, go for quality over quantity – have meat less often so you can afford better quality when you do have it. Avoid the cut-price meats in supermarkets and go for the highest quality you can afford; organic, free range ideally, to ensure good quality, nutritious meat.

TURKEY MEATBALLS IN TOMATO SAUCE

Serves 4

For the meatballs
500g turkey mince

2 jalapeños, finely chopped (optional)

1 onion, finely chopped

Salt and pepper

2 tsp mixed herbs

1 tsp coconut oil

For the tomato sauce
400g tin chopped tomatoes

2 tbsp tomato purée

2 cloves garlic, chopped

Salt and pepper

1 tbsp balsamic vinegar

1 tsp mixed herbs

To make the meatballs:

Mix all the ingredients (except the oil) together in a large bowl.

Using your hand, evenly divide the mixture into 4 portions and shape into meatballs.

Heat a teaspoon of coconut oil in a pan on a medium to high heat and place your meatballs in the pan.

Make sure you turn the meatballs regularly and cook for about 5 minutes each side or until cooked through.

To make the sauce:

Place the tinned tomatoes, tomato purée, garlic and seasoning in a pan and simmer for 10 minutes.

Add the balsamic vinegar and herbs and mix well.

Add the meatballs to the tomato sauce and simmer for approximately 20–30 minutes.

Tina says: These meatballs are also great served with sweet potato chips, a large green salad or a couple of slices of avocado. You can also make turkey burgers instead of meatballs with this recipe.

CLASSIC BOLOGNAISE

Serves 4

1 tbsp olive oil
1 small onion, finely chopped
1 clove garlic, crushed
500g lean minced beef
2 carrots, chopped
150g mushrooms, chopped
1 pepper, chopped
400g tin chopped tomatoes
1 tbsp tomato purée
1 tbsp balsamic vinegar
Salt and pepper
Sprinkle of chilli flakes (optional)

Heat the olive oil in a pan. Add the onion and garlic and cook for 2–3 minutes, until softened.

Add the mince and cook for a further 3–4 minutes, until browned.

Add the remaining vegetables, tinned tomatoes, tomato purée, balsamic vinegar, chilli flakes (if using) and seasoning.

Simmer on a low heat for 30–40 minutes until the sauce thickens.

Tina says: Add a handful of spinach right at the end for extra goodness!

LENTIL BOLOGNAISE

Serves 4

1 tbsp olive oil

1 onion, chopped

2 cloves garlic, finely chopped

1 red pepper, chopped

1 green pepper, chopped

400g tin chopped tomatoes

400g tin green lentils, drained

1 tbsp tomato purée

2 tsp dried basil

2 tsp dried oregano

150ml vegetable stock

Freshly ground pepper

Heat the olive oil in a large pan and fry the onion and garlic for 3–5 minutes until golden.

Add the peppers and continue frying for another minute, stirring frequently. Add the rest of the ingredients, bring to the boil and simmer for about 15 minutes.

Tina says: This could also be used to make a vegetarian shepherd's pie. Just pour the mixture into an ovenproof dish, top with mashed sweet potato and put in the oven at 180°C for about 30 minutes.

DAHL

Serves 4

200g green or yellow lentils
1 tbsp coconut oil
2 tsp mustard seeds
1 onion, finely chopped
1 tbsp ginger, finely chopped
2 cloves garlic, chopped
2 tsp ground cumin
1 tsp ground coriander
⅓ tsp ground turmeric
400g tin chopped tomatoes
1 tsp salt
100–200ml vegetable stock (if needed)
Juice of ½ lemon
Handful of fresh coriander

Pre-cook the lentils by boiling them in a saucepan full of water for about 15 minutes.

In a large pot, heat the coconut oil over a medium heat, then add the mustard seeds. Wait until the seeds pop – you will need to hold a lid just above the wok to stop them from popping all over the place.

Add the onion, ginger and garlic and fry for about 5 minutes until well browned.

Add the spices, stirring constantly for 30 seconds, and then add the tomatoes and salt. Drain the lentils and add them to the mixture. Bring to the boil and let simmer for about 20 minutes or until the

lentils are well cooked (this depends on the lentils you're using –
yellow ones tend to take longer than green ones). Add some stock
if needed (if the dahl gets very dry).

Take off the heat and add the lemon juice and coriander.

Serve with some brown rice.

BAKED SEA BASS

Serves 1

1–2 tsp olive oil
½ clove garlic, crushed
Salt and pepper
Chilli flakes
1 fillet sea bass
1 carrot, peeled and chopped
80g broccoli florets

Preheat the oven to 180°C.

In a bowl mix together the olive oil, crushed garlic, salt, pepper
and chilli flakes. Brush onto the sea bass fillet, wrap in tinfoil and
bake in the oven for approximately 30 minutes or until the fish is
cooked through.

Chop up the carrots and broccoli and steam for 5–7 minutes.

Serve with brown rice, sweet potatoes or baby potatoes.

CHICKEN STIR-FRY WITH ALMOND SATAY SAUCE

Serves 2

2 tbsp coconut oil

2 chicken fillets (about 250g), cut into chunks

3 spring onions, chopped

1 clove garlic, chopped

1 tbsp ginger, chopped

4 mushrooms, chopped

Handful of tender stem broccoli

½ red pepper, chopped

2 tbsp almond butter

2 tbsp tamari sauce

1 tbsp rice vinegar

4 tbsp water

⅓ tsp turmeric

Heat 1 teaspoon of coconut oil in a wok, add the chicken chunks and stir-fry for 5–8 minutes until well done. Put the chicken aside for a while.

Add another teaspoon of coconut oil to the wok, add the spring onions, garlic, ginger and mushrooms and stir-fry for 3 minutes. Add the broccoli and the pepper and stir-fry for another minute.

Add the almond butter, tamari sauce, rice vinegar, water and turmeric. Let the almond butter melt and mix well. Then add the chicken and mix. Cover and simmer for 5 minutes.

Serve with rice noodles (about 100g cooked noodles per person).

Tina says: You can leave out the mushrooms and try different dark green vegetables like kale and French beans. You could also try a different protein, such as king prawns. I like this cold too and tend to have leftovers as a snack the following day.

CHICKEN AND SWEET POTATO

Serves 1

200g sweet potato, peeled and chopped
2 tsp olive oil
1 medium chicken breast
Salt and pepper
1 carrot, peeled and sliced
80g broccoli

Preheat the oven to 180°C.

Wash and peel the sweet potato, chop into cubes or wedges, drizzle with the olive oil and place in the oven for about 50 minutes.

Season the chicken breast with a little salt and pepper. Wrap in tinfoil and bake in the oven for 35–40 minutes.

Steam the carrots and broccoli for about 5–7 minutes – there should still be a crunch in them when finished cooking.

CHICKEN SKEWERS

Serves 2

2 chicken breasts

1 courgette

1 pepper

8 button mushrooms

1 red onion

8 cherry tomatoes

½ tbsp coconut oil

Chop the chicken and the vegetables into chunks.

Melt the coconut oil and lightly coat the chicken with it. Season the chicken and the vegetables with herbs and spices of your choice.

Build the skewers by alternating between the chicken and the vegetables. Place under the grill on a high heat for 15–20 minutes, turning regularly.

Tina says: Try different vegetables or use monkfish or prawns instead of chicken (these will take less time to cook than the chicken). Turkey is also a great meat for these.

CHICKEN AND CASHEW NUT STIR-FRY

Serves 2

Rice noodles (approximately 100g cooked noodles per person)

2 chicken fillets (about 250g), cut into cubes

1 tbsp coconut oil

3 spring onions, chopped

2 cloves garlic, chopped

1 tbsp ginger, chopped

Handful of tender stem broccoli

½ red pepper sliced

1 tbsp rice vinegar

2 tbsp tamari sauce

2 tbsp water

2 tbsp cashew nuts

Cook the noodles according to the instructions on the packet and set aside.

Stir-fry the chicken in ½ tablespoon of coconut oil for 5–8 minutes until it's done and set aside.

Heat ½ tablespoon of coconut oil in a wok and stir-fry the spring onions, garlic and ginger for 2 minutes, then add the vegetables and the liquids and stir-fry for another minute.

Add the chicken, mix well, and continue stir-frying for another minute.

Add the cashew nuts and noodles and mix well until heated through.

Take off the heat and serve.

BEAN, LENTIL AND QUINOA HOTPOT

Serves 4

1 tbsp olive oil

1 onion, chopped

2 cloves garlic, chopped

1 red pepper, diced

½ courgette, finely chopped

100g red lentils

500ml water

2 tsp vegetable bouillon powder

7 peppercorns

1 tsp fennel seeds

1 tsp coriander seeds

2 carrots, diced

400g tin mixed beans (in water), drained

100g quinoa

400g tin chopped tomatoes

Tender stem broccoli (about 6 stems)

1–2 tbsp lemon juice

Salt

Handful of fresh coriander, chopped

Heat the olive oil in a pan and sauté the onion for 5 minutes.

Add the garlic, red pepper and courgette and continue cooking for 1 minute.

Add the lentils, water, bouillon powder, peppercorns, fennel seeds, coriander seeds, carrots and beans. Bring to the boil, then cover and simmer for about 10 minutes.

Add the quinoa, tomatoes and broccoli. Cover and simmer for another 15 minutes.

Season with the lemon juice and salt.

Remove from the heat and stir in the chopped coriander.

Serve on its own or with a spoonful of natural yoghurt.

BEAN BURGERS

Makes 10 medium burgers

400g tin cannellini beans, drained and rinsed

400g tin kidney beans, drained and rinsed

1 red onion, peeled and finely chopped

1 small (120g) sweet potato, peeled and grated

2 tbsp whole chia seeds

2 tbsp tahini

2 cloves garlic, finely chopped

2 tsp cumin

1 tbsp vegetable bouillon powder

Preheat the oven to 200°C and line a baking tray with greaseproof paper.

Place all the ingredients in a bowl, mix well with a spoon, then blend with a hand blender for 30–60 seconds, until the mixture is coarse.

Shape the mixture into balls, place on the baking tray and flatten with your fingers.

Bake for 15–20 minutes, until lightly coloured. Larger burgers may take up to 30 minutes to cook.

Tina says: These are fantastic with sweet potato chips, green salad and some hummus. One of my favourite dinners!

SPELT PIZZA

Serves 2–3

For the base
200g white spelt flour
1 tsp baking powder
1 tsp salt
1 tbsp milled chia seeds
2 tbsp olive oil
120–150ml warm water

For your toppings you could use a mixture of the following
Tomato sauce or red pesto
Buffalo mozzarella, sliced
Sliced mushrooms
Sweetcorn
Cherry tomatoes
Chopped peppers
Sliced courgette
Chopped spinach
Diced onions

To make the base: Mix the dry ingredients together, then add the olive oil and water little by little and mix well. If the mixture feels too dry add a bit more water. Knead for about 5 minutes. Cover with a tea towel and let the dough rest for 10–15 minutes.

Preheat the oven to 200°C.

Flatten the dough with your hands or a rolling pin.

On the base, spread pesto or tomato sauce, then add toppings, finishing with the sliced buffalo mozzarella.

Bake in the oven for about 15–20 minutes.

PESTO FRITTATA

Serves 2

6 sundried tomatoes (dried, not in oil)

½ red onion

½ red pepper

2 cloves garlic

5 mushrooms

4 eggs

3 tbsp natural yoghurt

3 tbsp red pesto

Freshly ground black pepper

1 tbsp olive oil

1 tsp mixed herbs

1 tsp dried basil

1 tbsp tamari sauce

½ ball buffalo mozzarella, thinly sliced

Prepare the sundried tomatoes according to the instructions on the packet.

Chop the onion, pepper, garlic and mushrooms.

Beat the eggs, then whisk together well the yoghurt, pesto and some freshly ground black pepper.

Heat the olive oil in a pan, add the onion, garlic and mushrooms and cook over a medium heat for 3–5 minutes. Add the red pepper and sundried tomatoes and cook for a further minute. Add the herbs and the tamari sauce. Cook for a further 2 minutes.

Pour in the eggs and cook over a medium heat until the frittata is firm. Add the sliced mozzarella and put the pan under a medium grill until the cheese has melted and the top is cooked well.

Tina says: I love this with sweet potato chips and a nice green salad.

QUINOA-STUFFED PEPPERS

Serves 2

1 tsp coconut oil
1 clove garlic, chopped
½ small onion, finely chopped
1 courgette, finely chopped
Salt and pepper
Pinch of chilli flakes (optional)
35g quinoa
2 red peppers
A little feta cheese

Heat the coconut oil in a pan, add the garlic and lightly sauté. Then add the onion and the courgette. Season with a little salt and pepper, and if you like add some chilli flakes for an extra kick. Continue to sauté for 10 minutes.

In another pan, cook the quinoa according to the instructions on the packet.

Once cooked, add the quinoa to the courgette, onions and garlic and mix together.

Slice your peppers in half and remove the seeds.

Divide the quinoa mixture between the peppers and crumble a little feta on top.

Cook in a preheated oven for 30 minutes at 180°C.

Tina says: Cook the quinoa in vegetable stock to make it tastier. You can use any other vegetables – mushrooms go nicely in this dish.

EASY THAI GREEN CURRY

Serves 4

1 tbsp coconut oil
500g chicken breasts, diced
2 tbsp Thai green curry paste*
1–2 red chillis, deseeded and diced
1 large courgette, chopped
120g mangetout
1 red pepper, chopped
1 yellow pepper, chopped
400ml coconut milk
Handful of cashew nuts

Heat the coconut oil in a pan.

Add the chicken and after a few minutes add a tablespoon of the curry paste.

Cook for a few more minutes and then add the vegetables.

Continue to cook for another 3 minutes, then pour in the coconut milk and add the other tablespoon of curry paste.

Bring to the boil, then turn down the heat and allow to simmer until the sauce has reduced slightly.

Serve with either brown rice or rice noodles and sprinkle some cashew nuts over the top.

* Please check the ingredients list on the curry paste. Many have sugar and other additives. Ideally get a good quality one from a health food shop.

SALMON AND SWEET POTATO CAKES

Serves 2

1 large sweet potato (approximately 180g)

1 salmon fillet (approximately 110g)

1 egg

Juice of ½ lemon

2 spring onions, chopped

2 tbsp ground almonds

Pinch of salt and pepper

Pinch of chilli flakes

Coconut oil for cooking

Preheat the oven to 180°C.

Wash the sweet potato and pierce the skin several times with a fork. Wrap in tinfoil and bake in the oven for approximately 40 minutes.

Wrap the salmon fillet in tinfoil and bake in the oven for about 15 minutes.

Once cooked, scoop the sweet potato out of its skin into a bowl and mash slightly. Flake the salmon fillet into the bowl with the sweet potato.

Add in the remaining ingredients (except the coconut oil) and combine with your hands, shaping the mixture into round 'cakes'.

If you find the mixture is too wet, add some more ground almonds.

Heat some coconut oil in a pan and fry the cakes on both sides over a medium heat for about 5 minutes or until golden.

Tina says: You can use tinned instead of fresh salmon.

CHICKEN GOUJONS

Serves 2

2 chicken breasts (approximately 250g)

1 egg, beaten

Salt and pepper

4 tbsp ground almonds

Coconut oil for cooking

Preheat the oven to 180°C.

Cut the chicken into strips.

Beat the egg in a bowl, add salt and pepper to season and mix together.

Dip each chicken strip into the egg, then roll in the ground almonds.

Fry in some coconut oil on a pan over a medium heat for a few minutes until they begin to brown.

Place the fried strips in the oven and bake for about 15–20 minutes.

CHICKPEA CURRY – CHANNA MASALA

Serves 4

1 tsp coconut oil

1 onion, finely chopped

2 cloves garlic, finely chopped

1 tbsp fresh ginger, finely chopped

1 red chilli, seeds removed and chopped (optional)

1 tsp cumin seeds

4 green cardamom pods, lightly crushed

1 tsp ground coriander

½ tsp turmeric

1 tsp garam masala

2 x 400g tins chopped tomatoes

1 tsp salt

2 x 400g tins chickpeas

Juice of ½ lemon

Handful of fresh coriander, chopped

Heat the coconut oil in a wok or a large pot over a medium heat. Add the onion and cook until lightly browned. Add the garlic, ginger and chilli, if using, and cook for another 2 minutes, stirring regularly.

Add the cumin, cardamon, ground coriander, turmeric and garam masala. Continue to cook for about 20–30 seconds until fragrant, stirring constantly. At this point, it is good to have a little water handy so that if you're worried about the spices burning, you can add some – you do not want the spices to burn, as the taste will be very unpleasant.

Add a small splash of water, about 30ml (if you haven't already done so), and cook until most of the water has evaporated.

Add the tomatoes and a teaspoon of salt and bring back to the boil. Cook for a couple of minutes, and then add the chickpeas, cover and let simmer for about 10 minutes.

Take 1 cup of the channa masala from the pot, put in a blender and blend until smooth. Pour the blended mixture back into the pot, mix well and cook for another minute.

Remove from the heat, squeeze in the lemon juice and add the chopped coriander. Stir well.

Serve with brown rice and some plain yoghurt.

Tina says: I love having leftovers on a slice of Ryvita the next day.

BLACKBEAN AND SWEET POTATO CHILLI

Serves 4

1 tsp coconut oil
1 small red onion, finely chopped
2 sticks celery, chopped
1 red pepper, finely chopped
1 clove garlic, chopped
2 tsp cumin seeds
2 tsp ground coriander
2 tsp paprika
½ tsp chilli powder (optional)
2 x 400g tins chopped tomatoes
1 tsp salt
400g tin black beans, drained and rinsed
1 medium-sized sweet potato, cut into small cubes
75g (½ cup) sweetcorn
Handful of fresh coriander, chopped
Juice of ½ lime

Heat the coconut oil in a wok or large pan, add the onion and celery and cook for a few minutes over a high heat until soft.

Reduce the heat to medium, add the red pepper and garlic and continue to cook for a few more minutes.

Add the spices, mix well and cook for a minute or so. You can add a splash of water to prevent the spices from burning (cooking them this way enhances the flavour but burning them will absolutely ruin the dish, so be careful!).

Add the tomatoes and salt, followed by the black beans and the sweet potato.

Mix well, cover and simmer on a low heat for about 45 minutes or until the sweet potato is well cooked (this depends on how small you chopped it).

Add the sweetcorn, cover and cook for another 2 minutes. Remove from the heat, add the coriander and lime juice and mix well.

Serve with brown rice.

Tina says: This is another dish that keeps well in the fridge and freezes well too. You can leave out the sweet potato and use another tin of black beans or kidney beans if you prefer.

CREAMY COURGETTE AND AVOCADO SPAGHETTI

Serves 2

2 tbsp cashew nuts

1 avocado, peeled and stoned

1 tbsp olive oil

Juice of ½ lemon

Salt and pepper

2–3 tbsp water

2 courgettes, made into spaghetti using a spiralizer or vegetable peeler

Half a ball of buffalo mozzarella, chopped into bite-size pieces

½ yellow pepper, chopped

Handful of cherry tomatoes, quartered

1 tbsp pine nuts

1 tbsp sunflower/pumpkin seeds

Sprinkle of nutritional yeast (optional)

Blend the cashew nuts in a blender. Once ground, add the avocado, olive oil and lemon juice and season with some salt and pepper. Add a little bit of water.

Blend, then add more water if you need to – this depends on how runny a consistency you want the sauce to have.

Make the courgettes into spaghetti. Place this in a bowl and add the mozzarella, pepper and tomatoes. Add your sauce and mix together.

Sprinkle the pine nuts and seeds on top and add a light sprinkle of nutritional yeast if using.

SIMPLE SALMON

Serves 1

1 salmon fillet
Juice of ½ lemon
Freshly ground black pepper

Preheat the oven to 180°C.

Put the salmon in an ovenproof dish, squeeze the lemon juice over it and sprinkle with freshly ground black pepper.

Cook in the oven for about 15 minutes. Cooking time depends on the size of the fillet, so check it regularly. Make sure you do not overcook salmon; for the best taste, you want it to be slightly pink in the middle.

Serve with stir-fried kale or leeks and sweet potato or brown rice.

Tina says: I love salmon. Buy good-quality fish, as you will notice the difference in taste and quality. Fish is best eaten immediately after cooking, not pre-cooked.

SIMPLE CHICKEN OR TURKEY

Serves 1

1 chicken or turkey breast
Juice of ½ lemon
Freshly ground black pepper

Preheat the oven to 180°C.

Place the chicken or turkey in an ovenproof dish, squeeze the lemon juice over it and grind over some black pepper.

Cook in the oven for about 20–25 minutes.

Tina says: Chicken is great in salads. I love it with a simple green salad, peppers, tomatoes and half an avocado.

TREATS

CRUNCHY STRAWBERRY DESSERT

Serves 1

1 tsp vanilla essence

5 tbsp natural yoghurt

6 strawberries, chopped

2 oatcakes per serving (Rough Oatcakes are great for this)

Stir the vanilla essence into the yoghurt until combined.

Chop the strawberries and mix them with the yoghurt.

Crumble the oatcakes and stir into the yoghurt mixture.

Tina says: This is a great quick treat to make when you fancy something sweet.

ALMOND AND COCONUT BISCUITS

Makes about 18

120g ground almonds

80g desiccated coconut

1 tsp vanilla essence

6 tbsp maple syrup

100g almond butter

Preheat the oven to 200°C.

Mix the dry ingredients together and then add everything else. Mix well. Use a food processor if you need to.

Once well mixed, take a large teaspoon of the dough, form into a ball and place on a lined baking tray. Flatten out if you need to. Repeat until all the dough has been used.

Bake in the oven for 8–10 minutes. Keep checking them to ensure they do not burn.

Tina says: Try adding some chopped dark chocolate or raisins to these to make them a special treat.

ALMOND BUTTER AND CHICKPEA COOKIES

Makes 14

400g tin chickpeas, drained and dried with kitchen paper
165g almond butter
1 tsp cinnamon
1 tsp baking powder
2 tsp vanilla essence
60ml (¼ cup) maple syrup
Handful of raisins

Preheat the oven to 180°C.

Blend everything except the raisins in a food processor until smooth.

Mix in the raisins.

Form into small balls with wet hands and flatten a bit with your fingers. Place on a lined baking tray.

Bake in the oven for about 10 minutes.

Allow to cool and enjoy!

Tina says: You'll never believe that these are actually healthy; they're so tasty!

CHIA SEED AND CACAO ENERGY BALLS

Makes 12

150g (½ cup) almond butter (or other nut butter)

1 tsp cinnamon

150ml (⅓ cup) maple syrup (or honey)

1 tbsp milled chia seeds

1 tbsp milled flaxseed

2 tbsp raw cacao powder

2 tbsp oats

Heat the nut butter, cinnamon and maple syrup in a pan for about a minute, until it softens and is easy to blend.

Add all the other ingredients and mix well. If the mixture is runny, let it cool and stiffen for a while.

Roll the dough into small balls with your hands.

Chill in the fridge for a couple of hours.

Store in an airtight container.

Tina says: These are so delicious I need to hide them because otherwise they'd be gone immediately!

AVOCADO CHOCOLATE MOUSSE

Serves 1

1 ripe avocado

32g (¼ cup) raw cacao powder

2 tbsp maple syrup

1 tsp vanilla essence

Blend all the ingredients together with a hand blender until smooth.

Add a bit more maple syrup if needed.

Tina says: Try adding some desiccated coconut or chopped almonds for variety.

HEALTHY BANANA SPLIT

Serves 1

1 banana
Natural yoghurt
Flaked almonds
Cashew nuts
Berries
Cinnamon

Slice the banana lengthways.

Dollop on some natural yoghurt and top with nuts and berries.

Sprinkle cinnamon over the top.

Add a drizzle of honey if you wish to make it sweeter.

Tina says: This makes a great dessert but I also like to have it for breakfast every now and then.

BANANA AND ALMOND BUTTER BITES

Serves 1–2

1 banana
Almond butter
Mixed chopped nuts

Slice the banana in half lengthways and smear the almond butter on top of each half.

Sprinkle the mixed chopped nuts on top and cut into bite-size pieces.

HEALTHY BBQ DESSERT

Serves 1

1 banana

Wrap an unpeeled banana in some tinfoil and place on the top part of the barbecue (the rack).

Turn occasionally until the skin has blackened.

Remove the peel and slice the banana in half, or alternatively just slice open the skin and scoop the gooey banana out with a spoon.

This is delicious served with natural or Greek yoghurt.

Tina says: This can also be done on a grill. You could also peel the banana, slice it in half and place it directly onto the grill or barbecue rack.

BANANA AND RASPBERRY 'ICE CREAM'

Serves 2

2 bananas, sliced and frozen

1 cup frozen raspberries

1 tsp vanilla essence or extract

Simply blend all the ingredients together in a processor or blender until smooth and creamy.

Serve sprinkled with chopped nuts.

APPLE CRISPS

Serves 1

1 apple (Pink Lady are great)

1 tbsp honey or maple syrup

Cinnamon

Preheat the oven to 180°C.

Core the apple, then slice into thin round slices.

Lightly coat the slices with some honey or maple syrup, using a pastry brush.

Lightly sprinkle with cinnamon (optional).

Bake in the oven for 15 minutes, then turn the slices over and cook for a further 15 minutes.

Allow to cool and enjoy.

STEWED APPLE

Makes 12 servings

1kg apples (Pink Lady are nice)
1 tsp coconut oil
1 tsp cinnamon

Core and chop the apples finely (no need to peel) and put them in a saucepan over a medium heat together with the coconut oil. Cover and let stew until the apples have softened. Add the cinnamon, let the apples cool a bit and blend until smooth.

Tina says: This is such a versatile dish. You can have it on its own to satisfy your sweet tooth, add it to your porridge, yoghurt or pancakes, or use to sweeten cakes. This freezes well and you could try adding some pear for extra sweetness.

SNACKS

CHOCOLATE-COVERED ALMONDS

Makes 4 servings

100g dark chocolate (minimum 75% cocoa)

½ tsp cinnamon

½ tsp vanilla essence

100g whole almonds

Put some water in a saucepan and bring to the boil, then reduce to a simmer. Put a heatproof bowl over the saucepan and put the chocolate in the bowl and let it melt. Once melted, add the cinnamon and vanilla essence and stir well.

Remove from the heat and add the almonds immediately. Stir well, ensuring all the almonds are covered in chocolate.

Scoop the almonds out with a spoon and put them on a sheet of baking paper. Put the baking paper on a large chopping board so you can easily move it.

Separate the almonds as much as possible and chill in the fridge until the chocolate hardens.

Tina says: This is a great snack that satisfies your chocolate cravings.

HEALTHY POPCORN

Makes 5 servings

2 tbsp coconut oil

100g (½ cup) corn kernels

Sea salt

Optional flavourings:

Nutritional yeast – gives a great 'cheesy' flavour while offering a boost of vitamin B12

Cinnamon

Cayenne pepper

Chilli flakes

Heat the coconut oil in a pan over a medium heat.

When the oil is hot, place the corn kernels in the pot, put a lid on and wait for it to start popping.

As the corn starts popping, shake the pot.

When popping slows and there are a couple of seconds in between each one, take the pot off the heat.

If you wish you can add an additional tablespoon of coconut oil to coat the popped corn – do this before adding any other flavourings.

Sprinkle with some sea salt and add your toppings.

Tina says: Be careful not to overheat the oil; keep it to a medium heat, as if it's too hot there will be a burnt taste. It took me a few tries to get this right before I realised I was overheating the oil.

LIME-TOASTED SUNFLOWER SEEDS

Makes 4 servings

100g sunflower seeds

2 tbsp tamari sauce

Juice of 1 lime

½ tsp maple syrup

½ tbsp coconut oil, melted

1 tbsp spelt flour

Heat a dry frying pan over a medium heat. Pour the seeds into the pan and toast until lightly browned, stirring regularly. This will take about 5–10 minutes.

Mix together all the other ingredients except the flour. Pour the mixture into the pan with the toasted seeds. Continue stirring for a few more minutes until all the liquid has evaporated. Remove from the heat and sprinkle in the flour, mixing well so that all seeds get covered in it. Pour onto a plate or baking sheet to cool.

Tina says: These are pretty tangy and remind me of salt and vinegar crisps only these are good for you! If you don't like the tanginess so much, just use a bit less lime.

BREAD

SPELT AND FLAXSEED SODA BREAD

Recipe by Rosanne Hewitt-Cromwell, author of Like Mam Used to Bake *(www.likemamusedtobake.com)*

Makes 2 loaves

375g wholemeal spelt flour
125g milled flaxseed
115g fine oatmeal
2½ tsp bicarbonate of soda
2 tsp salt
500ml buttermilk
2 tbsp honey

Preheat the oven to 220°C. Line two 2lb loaf tins with parchment paper – do not use greaseproof paper as the bread will stick to it.

Add all the dry ingredients to a large mixing bowl and give them a little stir with a wooden spoon.

Make a well in the centre of the dry ingredients and add the buttermilk and the honey. Stir with the wooden spoon until the ingredients are evenly mixed. Don't forget to get right down to the bottom of the bowl so that you don't miss any of the dry ingredients. At this stage the mixture will still seem quite wet, but don't worry about this, it is exactly how it should be.

Divide the mixture evenly between the 2 loaf tins. You can weigh it (approximately 630g per tin) or do this by eye, it's up to you. Score a line lengthways down the centre of each loaf with a sharp knife.

Place the loaf tins in the preheated oven and bake for 20 minutes, then reduce the temperature of the oven to 200°C and bake for a further 40 minutes.

Allow to cool slightly in the tins for 5 minutes before removing from the tins, removing the parchment paper and allowing to cool on a wire rack. Then, enjoy!

Rosanne says: You can buy fine oatmeal in health food shops. I don't always have time to get to a health food shop so I buy a pack of regular oats (porridge but not the instant stuff) and blitz them in the food processor. I do it with a 500g bag at a time to save having to do it every time I bake this bread.

APPENDIX 1 – WEEKLY PROGRESS CHART

I love nothing better than a good list or a chart, so here's a sample progress chart that you might want to use. All you have do is tick the box when you've done each listed item for the day.

	Mon	Tues	Wed	Thurs	Fri	Sat	Sun
Commit 100%							
Visualise							
Follow plan							
Keep food diary							
No sugar							
No processed foods							
No soft drinks							
Max 1 coffee							
No alcohol							
2 litres water							
Breakfast							
2 snacks							
Control portions							
Exercise							
Spend time outdoors							
Eat slowly							
Early night							
No TV							
No magazines							
Sit in silence							
Gratitude diary							
Think positive							

Note: you do not have to aim to do all of these every day of the week from day one. Start with small steps, e.g. aim to have one completely sugar-free day the first week, two the following week. Or aim for two early nights per week, one TV-free day, etc.